THE FAUST-LEGEND AND GOETHE'S 'FAUST'

BY

H. B. COTTERILL

EDITOR OF GOETHE'S 'IPHIGENIE'
SCHILLER'S 'LAGER' 'SELECTIONS
FROM THE NIBELUNGENLIED' DANTE'S
'INFERNO' ETC.

LONDON
GEORGE G. HARRAP & COMPANY
9 PORTSMOUTH STREET KINGSWAY W.C.
1912

BALLANTYNE & COMPANY LTD
TAVISTOCK STREET COVENT GARDEN
LONDON

Printing Statement:

Due to the very old age and scarcity of this book,
many of the pages may be hard to read due to the
blurring of the original text, possible missing pages,
missing text, dark backgrounds and other issues
beyond our control.

Because this is such an important and rare work, we
believe it is best to reproduce this book regardless of
its original condition.

Thank you for your understanding.

PREFACE

THESE lectures have been given perhaps half a dozen times, in England, in Switzerland and in Germany. On allowing them to appear in print I should perhaps apologize to my readers for the somewhat free and familiar style in which parts of them are written; but even if I had the time to recast them into a more serious form I should be unwilling to do so, for there is surely enough ponderous literature on the subject, and although some may resent in a book what often helps to make a lecture attractive, I think I can rely on the fact that many people agree with the dictum of Horace:

Ridiculum acri
Fortius et melius magnas plerumque secat res,

or, as Milton has it:

Joking decides great things
Stronger and better oft than earnest can.

Almost the only change that I have made in my MS. has been the substitution or

PREFACE

addition of an English translation in numerous places where I had formerly quoted the German original. On some occasions, when first writing the lectures, I very probably used the English version of *Faust* by Bayard Taylor, but I have not the book at present at hand and cannot feel quite certain whether any of the verse translations are not my own. The little book makes of course no pretence to be a contribution to critical or biographical literature. It is meant especially for those who wish to know something more about the story of Faust and about Goethe's play, and who, because their knowledge of German does not suffice or for other reasons, are unable to study the subject in any more satisfactory way.

H. B. C.

FREIBURG IM BREISGAU
August 1912

CONTENTS

I

THE OLD FAUST-LEGEND

ALL of us have probably experienced the fact that it is possible to have been familiar for a long time with some great work of imagination—some poem or picture—to have learnt to love it almost as if it were a living person, to imagine that we understand it and appreciate it fully, even to fancy that it has a special message, a deeper meaning, for us than for almost any one else, and then to come across somebody—some commentator perhaps—who informs us that our uncritical appreciation is quite worthless, mere shallow sentiment, and that until we can accurately analyze and formulate the Idea which the artist endeavoured to incorporate in his work, and classify the diverse manifestations of this Idea as subjective, objective, symbolical, allegorical, dramatical-psychological or psychological-dramatical,

9

we are not entitled to hold, far less to express, any opinion on the subject.

When I realised that I had undertaken to lecture on *Faust*, I thought it my duty to study Goethe's German commentators— some of them at least; for to study all would consume a lifetime. A few of the works of these commentators I already possessed—some, I am sorry to say, with their pages yet uncut. Others I procured, following the advice of German friends well versed in the matter. I set to work on what was presumably the best of these commentaries. As I laboured onwards, page after page, I found myself from time to time turning back to the title of the book. Sure enough, it was *Ueber Goethe's Faust*. I laboured on—the suspicion deepening at every turn of the page that perhaps the binder might have bound up the wrong text under the title *Ueber Goethe's Faust*. At the fifty-third page I came to a dead stop. Except quite incidentally neither Goethe nor Faust had as yet been mentioned. These fifty-three pages had been entirely devoted to what seemed to my rather unmetaphysical mind a not very luminous or edifying dissertation on the difference between *Ansicht*

10

and *Einsicht*—between mere Opinion and
true critical Insight; and, as far as I could
discover, the only conclusion as yet arrived
at was that the writer possessed an exclu-
sive monopoly in the last-mentioned article.

But I will not inflict upon you any
further description of my tusslings ·with
Teutonic interpreters of *Faust*—with their
egos and *non-egos*, their moral-æsthetic
symbolisms and so on. Let us leave them
to the tender mercies of Goethe himself,
who was not sparing of his ridicule in regard
to his commentators, nor, alas, at times in
regard to his countrymen. ' Of all nations,'
he says, ' the Germans understand me least.
. . . Such people make life a burden by their
abstruse thoughts and their *Ideas*, which
they hunt up in all directions and insist on
discovering in everything. . . . They come
and ask *me* what " Ideas " *I* have incor-
porated in my *Faust*. Just as if I myself
knew !—or could describe it, even if I did
know !' Of course Goethe's great poem
contains an Idea, if by that word we mean in
a poem what we mean by *life* in anything
living; but it is not by dissection and
analysis that we shall discover it. ' He who
wishes,' says Goethe in *Faust*, ' to examine

11

and describe anything living first does his best to expel the life. Then he has got the dead parts in his hand ; but what is wanting is just the spiritual bond.' It is my purpose —a purpose not easy of fulfilment—to avoid this method of dissection and to place before you living realities, not anatomical specimens.

But before we plunge *in medias res* and grapple our present subject, namely the old Faust-legend, I should like to say just a few words in order to show from what standpoint I think we should regard Goethe as a poet and a thinker—for that he is great both as a poet and as a thinker cannot be denied.

Goethe describes his own philosophy as the philosophy of action. He believed in impulse, in inspiration, in action, rather than in reflexion, analysis and logic. 'Reflect not!' he makes Iphigenie exclaim—'Reflect not! Grant freely as thou feel'st!' And in one of his Epigrams he says:

> *Yes, that's the right way,*
> *When we cannot say*
> *How we think. True thought*
> *Comes as a gift, unsought.*

Such theory of inspiration is thoroughly

12

Greek, reminding one of Plato's 'muse-inspired madman' and of what Sophocles is related to have said to Aeschylus: 'Thou, Aeschylus, always dost the right thing—but unconsciously (ἀλλ' οὐκ εἰδώς γε).' Thus it was also with Goethe. All intellectual hobbies and shibboleths, all this endless wearisome discussion and dissection and analysis and criticism and bandying about of *opinion*, which is the very life-breath of modern intellectual existence and modern journalistic literature, Goethe rejected, as Plato had done in his *Phaedrus*, where he makes Socrates call such things 'rotten soul-fodder.'

'The whole! The whole!' was Goethe's frequent exclamation—'life! action! being! —the living whole, not the dead parts!' He was for ever decrying mere thought, mere intellect, mere cleverness. And yet of all moderns what greater intellect, what greater thinker, can we name than Goethe himself? Seldom, perhaps never, has there existed a mortal so many-sided. 'In such manifold directions'—he wrote to his friend Jacobi—'does my nature move, that I cannot be satisfied with *one* single mode of thought. As poet and artist I am polytheist; as a

13

student of Nature I am pantheist. When I need a God for my personal nature, as a moral and spiritual human being, He also exists for me. Heaven and earth are such an immense realm that it can only be grasped by the collective intelligence of all intelligent beings.' Such 'collective intelligence' Goethe perhaps more nearly possessed than any other human being has done. The lordly pleasure-house which he built for his soul was such as Tennyson describes (and his words refer of course to Goethe):

> *Full of great rooms and small the palace stood,*
> *All various, each a perfect whole*
> *From living Nature, fit for every mood*
> *And change of my still soul.*

And wonderfully true are those other lines of Tennyson—but rather bitter, as perhaps was to be expected of Tennyson when he was describing a great character with which he had so little sympathy:

> *I take possession of man's mind and deed.*
> *I care not what the sects may brawl.*
> *I sit as God holding no form of creed,*
> *But contemplating all.*

To Goethe all things both in Nature and in

Art were but transitory reflexions of the real and eternal. 'Alles vergängliche ist nur ein Gleichnis'—all things transitory are but a parable, an allegory of truth and reality—such are some of the last words of his great Poem; and thus too he regarded his own poetry. 'I have,' he said, 'always regarded all that I have produced as merely symbolic, and I did not much care whether what I made were pots or dishes' Even that life-poem of his, *Faust*, which he planned and began as a young man of about twenty-five, and the last lines of which he wrote a few months before his death, aged eighty-two, only represents (as indeed do all great works of art) *one* aspect of belief—or perhaps I should rather say a certain number of truth's innumerable aspects, none of them claiming to afford a full vision, and not a few of them apparently contradictory; for, as both Plato and Shakespeare tell us, truth cannot be directly stated : it lies, as it were, in equipoise between contradictory statements :

For no thought is contented. The better sort,
As thoughts of things divine . . . do set the word
Against the word.

Faust does not claim to be a universal

Gospel, nor to offer a final solution of the riddle of existence. It makes no attempt to pile up Pelions on Ossas—to scale heaven with the Babel-towers of the human reason. It merely holds up a mirror in which we see reflected certain views of truth, such as presented themselves to Goethe from some of his intellectual heights. To regard it and judge it otherwise—to analyse its Idea —to insist on discovering its Moral—to compare it with some little self-contained system of theory or dogma which we ourselves may have finally accepted—and to condemn Goethe as a prophet of lies because, viewing truth from such diverse standpoints (many of them perhaps quite inaccessible for us) he may seem at times to ignore some of our pet formulæ—this, I think, would convict us of a lamentable lack of wisdom and humility. And if at times we feel pained by what may seem irreverent, let us remember that Goethe wrote also these words : ' With many people who have God constantly on their tongues He becomes a phrase, a mere name uttered without any accompanying idea. If they were penetrated by God's greatness, they would rather be dumb and for very reverence not dare to name Him.

16

Goethe accepted not without a certain amount of pride the title given him by some of his contemporaries—that of 'the last of the Heathen.' But which of us will doubt the sincerity or fail to be touched by the humility of his words : 'And yet perhaps I am such a Christian as Christ Himself would wish me to be.'

There are doubtless but very few (and I confess that I am not one of these select few) who can accept Goethe in all his many-sidedness. We ordinary mortals are incapable of such Protean versatility and are sure to find points, often many and important points, where we are strongly repelled by his teachings and his personality. The idealist is scandalized by his vigorous realism, the realist and materialist by his idealism, the dogmatist by his free thought, the free-thinker by his reverence towards religion, while the scientific expert is apt to regard him as a mere poet, oblivious or ignorant of the fact that, although without scientific training, besides propounding theories on Colour which were for a time accepted by leading authorities on that subject and besides making a discovery which had escaped the investigations of professional

Anatomists (that of the intermaxillary bone), Goethe was the discoverer of a law, that of the metamorphosis of leaves and flowers, which may be said to have almost revolutionised the science of Botany.

Let us now turn to our subject and attempt to trace to its first sources this strange and suggestive legend of Faust, the great Magician.

And first, we shall see our way more clearly if we consider what is really the nature of that magic, or black art, which played such an important part in the medieval imagination.

Perhaps we may say that by ' magic ' was denoted that art by which one was supposed to gain a knowledge of, and a power over, the prime elements of Nature and its cosmic potencies, so as to be able to combine and use them independently of natural laws. It is this power that Faust in Goethe's play longs to attain :

> . . . *To find the force*
> *That binds the world and guides its course,*
> *Its germs and vital powers explore*
> *And peddle with worthless words no more.*

In almost every age and nation we find

a vital Power, an ordering Force, recognised as present in the natural world, and the human mind seems ever prone to believe such Power to have affinity to human nature and to be, so to speak, open to a bargain. The fetish priest, the rain doctor, the medicine-man, the Hindu yogi, the Persian Mage, the medieval saint, and countless miracle-workers in every age, have ever believed themselves to be, whether by force of will, or by ecstatic contemplation, or by potent charms, in communion with the great Spirit of Nature, or with mighty cosmic influences—with Powers of Light or of Darkness; with Oromasdes or Arimanes, Brahma or Siva, Jehovah or Baal; with Zoroastrian Devs, Persian Genii, guardian angels or attendant demons; with the Virgin Queen of heaven—whether as Selene, Astarte, Hecate, or the Madonna; with the Prince of the powers of this world —with or without his horns and his cloven foot.

Not only among the heathen—the orientals and Egyptians—but also among the Chosen People we find the priests attesting their favour with the Deity, and asserting the truth of their religion, by what we

may call orthodox magic. We all re-
member how Aaron's rod, in the form of
an orthodox snake, swallowed up the
unorthodox rod-snakes of the Egyptian
sorcerers, and how Elijah attested the
power of the true God by calling down fire
from heaven in his contest with the priests
of the Sun-god Baal. King Solomon too
was for many ages credited with magic
powers and was regarded in medieval
times as the great authority in matters of
wizardry.

Among the Greeks, although mysteries
and witches played no small part in the old
religion and survived long in popular super-
stition, magic was thrust into the back-
ground by the poetic and philosophic
Hellenic imagination. The powers of
Nature were incorporated in the grand and
beautiful human forms of the Olympian
gods, or in the dread shapes of the Infernal
deities. But even among those of the
Greeks who were raised far above the
ordinary superstitions of the populace we
find many traces of mysticism and magic,
as for example in connexion with oracles,
with divine healing, with the efficacy of
images and other sacred objects, and espe-

cially in connexion with Orphic and other Mysteries. And, while for the most part Greek philosophy was rather imaginative than mystic, still we encounter the genuine mystic element in such Greek sages as Empedocles and Pythagoras, both of whom assumed the priestly character and seem to have laid claim to supernatural powers. Empedocles indeed, it is said, gave himself out to be a deity exiled from heaven, and was apparently worshipped as such. According to a not very trustworthy legend he threw himself into the crater of Mount Etna—perhaps in order thus to solve the mystery of existence. Pythagoras is said by some to have met his death at the hands of the people of Crotona, who set fire to his house and burnt him alive with many of his disciples. Goethe evidently alludes to Pythagoras (as well perhaps as to John Huss and others who found their death at the stake) in some well-known lines, which may be roughly thus translated :

The few that truth's deep mystery have learned
And could not keep it in their hearts concealed,
But to the mob their inner faith revealed,
Have evermore been crucified and burned.

21

THE FAUST-LEGEND

We now come to Christianity. In the early ages of the Church the final appeal seems to have been an appeal to miracles, and we find the apostles and their followers claiming the sole right of working miracles in the name of the one true God and anathematizing all other wonder-workers as in league with Satan. We all remember Elymas the Sorcerer struck blind by St. Paul, and the adversary of St. Peter, Simon the Mage, around whom first gathered the myths which lived so long in the popular imagination and many of which we shall meet with in the legend of Dr. Faust.

This Simon, the Magus or Sorcerer, who bewitched the people of Samaria, and was looked upon as 'the great power of God,' is said in the *Acts of the Apostles* to have been converted by St. Philip and to have brought upon himself a severe rebuke from St. Peter for offering to purchase with money the gift of wonder-working. In about the third century the legend of Simon Magus, as related by Clement of Alexandria, seems to have already incorporated in a mythical form the discords of the early Church, and especially the feud between the Jewish Christians, followers of

22

St. Peter, and the Gentile proselytes, followers of St. Paul. Indeed Simon the Sorcerer was in course of time regarded by some as having been identical with St. Paul—that is to say, it was believed that St. Paul had been none other but Simon Magus in disguise. The voice heard at St. Paul's conversion and the light by which for a season he was struck blind were alleged to have been feats of wizardry by which he, a wolf in sheep's clothing, stole his way into the true fold in order to introduce discord and to betray the Church to the Gentiles.

St. Peter, the true Simon, is said to have followed the false Simon from city to city, out-rivalling his Satanic miracles by orthodox miracles, until at length they reached Rome. Here Simon Magus by his magic arts succeeded in flying up into the sky in the presence of the Emperor and his court, but at the word of Peter the charm was broken and the wizard fell to earth and was killed.

But, besides this, the so-called Gnostic heresy introduced other elements into the legend. These Gnostics were a sect that arose in the early times of Christianity. They pretended to a special insight into the divine nature, and combined Platonic and oriental theories with Christian dogmas. They tried to convert the story of the Redemption into a cosmological myth, and regarded the human person of Christ as a kind of phantom—a magic apparition. Some of these Gnostics seem to have accepted Simon Magus as the 'Power of God'—as the Logos, or divine Reason, by which the world was created (or reduced from chaos to an ordered Cosmos). From this a curious myth arose. This Logos, or creative Power, was identified with the Sun-god, as the source of life, and as Sun-god was united to the Moon-goddess, Selene. Now the words Helen and Selene are connected in Greek, and Helen of Troy was accepted by these Gnostics as a mythical form of the goddess of the moon. Hence it came that in the Gnostic form of the Simon Magus legend he was married to Helen of Troy, and this notion found its way into the old Faust-legend, and is used by Goethe in that exceedingly wonderful and beautiful part of his great poem which is called the *Helena*.

After the suppression of Gnostic and other early heresies came the contest of the

24

now united and politically powerful Church
against the outer world of heathendom.
While retaining for herself what we may
call a monopoly in orthodox magic the
Church condemned as in league with the
devil *all* speculation, whether theological or
scientific—the one as leading to heresy, the
other to sensual ends, such as riches, fame,
and those lusts of the flesh and that pride
of intellect which were fatal to the contem-
plative and ascetic ideals of medieval
Christianity.

It was not among Teuton and Celtic
savages but among the learned adherents of
the old Greek philosophy that the Church
in those earlier days found her most danger-
ous and obstinate adversaries. Plato and
Aristotle (whose tenets the Christian
Schoolmen afterwards endeavoured to har-
monize with the teaching of the Gospel)
were at first brought forward to oppose the
new religion, these doctrines of Greek
philosophy being largely supplemented by
mystic ideas derived from oriental sources.
It was however Pythagoras, the great
Greek-Italian philosopher of the sixth
century B.C., the predecessor and to some
extent the inspirer of Socrates and Plato,

who was most generally accepted as the rival of St. Paul. It was his mystical doctrines of Number and Harmony, of the Unit and the Triad, which were most often marshalled against the Christian doctrine of the Unity and Trinity of the Godhead. Indeed it even seems that Pythagoras was believed by some of these adversaries of Christianity to be the incarnation of Deity (as had been believed in his lifetime) and to be the friend and saviour of mankind, like Prometheus of old, who was said to have given his life for the human race devoted to destruction by the anger of an offended God.

No wonder that, embittered by such opponents, the Church launched her anathema against all the profane learning of the day—all study of the ancient heathen philosophers and poets. The gods of Olympus became synonymous with demons and monsters of the Christian hell, as we see in Dante and in such old legends as that of the Hill of Venus. Plato and Aristotle, and even Homer, were put on the index. Virgil especially was regarded as a dangerous wizard—although in another age he was honoured almost as a prophet and a foreteller of the Messiah. I remember that many years ago, when I was searching for Virgil's tomb on Posilipo near Naples, I was informed by a contadino, of whom I had asked my way, that Virgil ('Marone,' as he called him) was a great magician. The man knew nothing of Virgil as poet. Probably Virgil's account of the descent of Aeneas into the lower world, and that strange *Eclogue* of his, the *Pollio*, in which possibly a Sibylline prophecy of the coming of a Messiah is reproduced, may have credited him with magic lore, and may also have invested him for a time with almost the dignity of a canonical Minor Prophet.

Now, during these ante-Reformation ages the Roman Church claimed, as I have said, a monopoly in orthodox magic. She could send a soul to hell, or by rites and exorcism she could save the sinner from his compact with Satan, as one sees in such legends as those of Merlin, of Tannhäuser, of Robert the Devil, and of that Theophilus who was converted by flowers sent him from Paradise by the Virgin-Martyr St. Dorothea. Of another Theophilus, an eastern monk of perhaps the sixth century, we are told that,

27

like Faust, he made a written compact with the devil, but repented and was saved by the Virgin Mary, who snatched the fatal document from the devil's claws and gave it back to the penitent.

But there is one early example of the wizard-legend where the magician is saved from his pact with Satan not so much by the counter-charms of the Church as by the purity and steadfastness of Christian maidenhood, and for this reason I think the poet Shelley is right in regarding this legend as ' the true germ of Goethe's *Faust*.' It is the story of Cyprian and Justina, who were among the many victims of the persecution of the Christians by Diocletian, about 300 A.D. Cyprian was a sorcerer of Antioch whose diabolical arts failed to overcome the sanctity of Justina. He confessed himself conquered and withdrew into the desert as a Christian hermit. The story has been dramatized by the Spanish poet Calderon in his *Magico Prodigioso*, a part of which has been finely translated by Shelley. The beautiful picture of St. Justina by Moretto, where Cyprian is kneeling before her and a white unicorn, the symbol of chastity, is crouching in the foreground, is well known.

28

AND GOETHE'S 'FAUST'

With the Reformation another spirit arose
and legends took a different form. In the
Protestant world the orthodox magic of the
Roman Church lost its saving power and was
regarded as no less diabolic than all other
black art. He was irretrievably lost who
had once given over his soul to magic and
the devil (and the devil was at this time, as
we know, a very real personage—real enough
to have an inkpot hurled at his head by
Luther). The revival at the Renaissance of
speculation and research, combined as it was
with all kinds of fantastic hopes of discover-
ing prime matter, the ' Philosopher's stone,'
and elixirs of life, bred in the popular super-
stition a mysterious awe and attached to
almost all scientific investigation the epithet
' black,' or diabolic, as opposed to the ' white
art' of holding communion with good spirits.
Alchemy and astrology (words meaning
merely what we call chemistry and astro-
nomy) became words of hellish import, and
he who practised these arts was in league
with Satan. Thus were regarded such men
as Lully, Roger Bacon, the Abbot Tritheim,
and (perhaps best known of all, at least to all
readers of Browning) Bombastes Paracelsus,
the contemporary of Faust, born at Einsie-

29

deln, between Brunnen and the lake of Zürich, in the year 1493.

Thus the sixteenth-century form of our legend is of the most tragic character. In the oldest Faust-legend, which first took shape in this century, there is no hint of his being saved. And another of its characteristics is its strong anti-papal tendency. The devil appears in the guise of a monk, and even as Mahomet or Antichrist in the guise of the Pope himself.

But the Renaissance (if not the Reformation) introduced another, entirely new and most important, element into the legend—one which enabled Goethe to use the sulphurous old myth as the subject for a great poem. Not only was there a renaissance of learning, but also of art—an intense longing for both Knowledge and Beauty. To *know* everything—to learn the inner secret of Nature—to understand, as Faust longed to understand,

The inmost force
That binds the world and guides its course—

this yearning after perfection by Knowledge was one of the fruits of the Renaissance. The other was the yearning to gain perfection by means of *feeling*, by the ecstatic contemplation of and communion with perfect Beauty—'to love infinitely and be loved,' as Aprile says in Browning's *Paracelsus*. These two impulses, the one toward Knowledge and the other toward Love, were doubtless awakened by the study of Aristotle, that 'master of those who know,' and of Plato's doctrine of the soul's love-inspired yearnings for Truth and Beauty and for communion with the Perfect and the Eternal.

I have called them *two* impulses, and to the mind they must ever appear distinct, nay sometimes contrary; but I need not remind you how Christianity teaches us to reconcile the ancient feud between the mind and the heart—between Knowledge and Love. You may perhaps remember how Dante, to intimate to us that there can be no true knowledge without love and no true love without knowledge, speaks of the Cherubim and the Seraphim as ideally the same, and tells us that the Seraphs, who love most, also know most.

Both these impulses are noble and awaken our sympathy.

Now, in order that *tragic* art may have its effect it must possess what Aristotle calls πάθος, so that we may be able to sympathize

with the sufferer. Thus, for instance, Milton
enlists our sympathies even with his Satan,
and it is perhaps because we cannot sym-
pathize in any way with Dante's Lucifer that
many feel repelled by the terrible creation.
But even in the oldest of the Faust-legends,
and far more of course in Goethe's *Faust*, we
are attracted by a 'pathetic' element, viz.,
the unsatisfied and insatiable longing of a
human soul for Knowledge--for Truth--and
its still intenser yearnings after ideal Beauty.

Thus, even the Faust of the older sixteenth-
century legend, although he ultimately falls
a victim to the devil, has noble and high
impulses by which we feel strongly attracted.
He is lost, not through these impulses, these
yearnings for knowledge, but through his
magic, and his sensual life. In spite of more
than one fit of remorse he is unable to free
himself from the lusts of the flesh; he is
obliged to sign a second bond with Mephisto
and is dragged down ever lower into the
abyss, until the jaws of hell open and swallow
him up—while the Faust of Goethe's poem
gains strength through many an error, and
many a grievous fall, gradually shakes off
the diabolic influence and rising on the step-
ping-stones of his dead self is finally rescued

32

by God's mercy and reaches the higher spheres of another life.

How infinitely grander—how illimitable in its vistas—the subject becomes when thus treated by a great poet we all must feel. And even if we cannot with a whole heart accept as a true Gospel what (in spite of Goethe's admission that God's mercy was a necessary factor) seems to be a gospel of *self-salvation*, we should not forget that this picture of a man pressing on in his own strength amidst the lusts of the flesh and the errors of the mind is perhaps the noblest and grandest kind of picture that dramatic art can offer us—that of the human will in its struggle against destiny. In any case, I think, we cannot refuse our sympathy for these yearnings and searchings for truth amidst error. Do you remember what Lessing said about such longings ? 'If God' —he said—' should hold Truth itself in His right hand, and in His left the longing for Truth, and should say to me *Choose !* I would humbly fall down before His left hand and say : *Father, pure Truth is for Thee alone. Give me the longing for Truth, though it be attended with never-ending error.*'

There seems no doubt that a man named

Johann Faust, renowned for his learning and credited with magical powers, actually did exist—probably about 1490 to 1540. (He was therefore a contemporary of Paracelsus, and also of Luther, Charles V., Henry VIII. and Raphael.) Several notices of this Dr. Johann Faust occur in writers of the period. One of the most circumstantial is by the friend and biographer of Melanchthon, who himself seems to have met Faust. But the various myths that gathered round the magician were, it seems, first published in a continuous narrative in 1587, that is about fifty years after his death. This is the old *Frankfurter Faustbuch*, of which only one perfect specimen is now known to exist. It is, I believe, in Leipzig. A mutilated copy is in the Vienna Library.

One day, when to escape for a time from the German commentators above mentioned I had gone out for a walk, I found my way to the old Wasserkirche— now the Free Library of the city of Zürich, and here I discovered a facsimile reprint of this old Frankfurt Faust-book. As this is the oldest and most authentic basis of all later forms of the story and is doubtless the one which (as well as the puppet-play on the subject) Goethe used

as the ground-plan for his poem, I perhaps
cannot do better than give a brief abstract
of its contents.

It is written in quaint old German and is
interspersed with many pious comments,
biblical quotations and Latin words and
phrases, and now and then it breaks out
into doggerel verse. The editor (Spiess by
name) tells us that he publishes the book
s a warning to all Christians and sensible
people to avoid the terrible example of
Doctor Faustus.' He evidently takes the
thing very seriously and has purposely (as
he says) omitted all 'magic formulæ,' lest
any should by this Historia be incited to
inquisitiveness and imitation.' Johann Faust,
according to this version, was born at Roda,
a village near Weimar. (Other versions say
at Knittlingen in Würtemberg.) His parents
were honest God-fearing peasants. His
great abilities induced a rich relation in
Wittenberg to adopt and educate him. He
studied theology at Wittenberg (known to
us all through Hamlet and Luther) and also
at Cracow, outrivalling all competitors and
gaining the title of Doctor of Theology.
But he had not only a 'teachable and quick'
but also a 'foolish, silly, inquisitive' head,

35

and neglecting the Bible became a 'Speculator' and prided himself more on being an Astrologus and a Mathematicus than a Theologus. As the old chronicler expresses it, he 'took to himself eagle's wings and desired to search out the reasons of all in heaven and on earth.'

He now takes to 'Zauberei'—magic. Where four roads meet in the Spessart Wald, a forest near Wittenberg, he inscribes mystic circles and performs incantations for the purpose of summoning the devil. After all kinds of fearful apparitions and noises, by which Faust is almost terrified to death, a demon appears in the shape of a 'grey monk.' Faust invites him to visit him at his house in Wittenberg. The demon visits him there and tells him of all the horrors of hell. But Faust persists in his plan and makes a second rendezvous with the demon, who has now procured leave from his lord and master Lucifer to offer his services and attendance. The compact is made. The demon is to serve him for twenty-four years. Faust is to renounce Christianity and to hate all Christians, and at the end of twenty-four years he is to belong to the demon 'to have power, rule and dominion over his soul,

36

body, flesh, blood, and possessions, and that
for all eternity.' This compact has to be
signed with blood. Faust pierces his hand,
and the blood flows out and forms the words
' O homo fuge!'—'O man, escape!'—but
Faust, though alarmed, is not deterred. It
is now agreed that the demon shall appear,
whenever summoned, in the form of a
Franciscan monk. He then reveals his name:
Mephistopheles, or, as the old legend gives
it, Mephostophiles—the meaning of which
is probably 'not loving the light'—$\mu\grave{\eta}$ $\phi\hat{\omega}\varsigma$
$\phi\iota\lambda\hat{\omega}\nu$—a compound which you may rightly
remark must have been concocted by a
rather second-rate Greek scholar.

After a season of dissipation, during which
Faust is supplied with all the luxuries that
he desires—wine stolen from ducal, electoral,
and episcopal cellars, soft and costly raiment
from the draperies and naperies of Nürnberg
and Frankfurt and so on (he had, for
instance, only to open his window and call
any bird, goose, turkey, or capon, and it
would at once fly in, ready roasted)—
getting tired of this kind of thing he falls
in love and wishes to marry. But Mephisto
angrily tells him that marriage is a thing
pleasing to God and against the terms of

the compact. You will notice here the Lutheran and anti-papal tendency—marriage being a thing pleasing to God in itself, and any compact being devilish which forbade it, as in the case of priests and monks.

Then follow long discussions and disputations between Faust and Mephisto on the creation of the world, on hell and heaven, and on black art and astrology. None of us may be in a position to question a demon's accuracy with regard to how affairs stand in Hades, but Mephisto gives a very unorthodox account of the creation—or rather he denies that there was any creation. Matter according to his theory (and it is a theory of some modern scientists and not only of medieval demons)—matter is eternal and self-existent—uncreated, or self-created, whatever that may mean. Incited by these descriptions, and by his ' foolish silly inquisitive head,' Faust demands that he should pay a visit to both hell and heaven.

For the journey to Hell the services of Beelzebub have to be requisitioned. The devilish worm, as the old writer calls Beelzebub, places Faust in a chair or pannier made of bones, hoists the chair on to his back and plunges (like Empe-

docles) into a volcano. Faust is nearly
stifled to death. He sees all kinds of
griffins and monsters and great multitudes
of spirits tormented in the flames—among
them emperors, kings and princes. Then
in a deep sleep he is brought home and laid
on his bed. ' This Historia and recount of
what he saw in hell,' says the old chronicler,
'hath Doctor Faustus himself written down
with his own hand, and after his death it
was found lying in a sealed book.' After this
(about ten years of the twenty-four having
already elapsed) he is taken up to heaven
by Mephisto in a chariot drawn by
dragons—not of course to the Empyrean,
the abode of God, but up as far as the fixed
stars (the eighth sphere). He finds the sun,
which before he had believed to be only as
big as the bottom of a cask, to be far
larger than the earth, and the planets to be
as large as the earth, and the clouds of the
upper sky to be as dense and hard as rocks
of crystal. From these regions the earth
looks as small as the ' yolk in an egg.' He
sees all the kingdoms of the earth—Europe,
Asia, and Africa (not America, although
America was discovered by Columbus in
1492, about the date of Faust's birth).

THE FAUST-LEGEND

In the sixteenth year Faust wishes to
pay a visit to the chief cities and countries
of the world. Mephisto changes himself
into a horse—'with wings like a drome-
dary.' It is, I believe, not generally sup-
posed that a dromedary has wings ; but I
suppose the old chronicler must have
confused a camel and an ostrich, thinking
of the name which some Greek authors
give to the ostrich, namely *stroutho-camelos*
or ' sparrow-camel.'

On the back of his sparrow-camel horse
Faust is carried through the air to many
lands and cities and at length reaches
Rome, and visits the Pope, on whom he
and Mephisto (both being invisible) play
various practical jokes, blowing in his face,
snatching his food away at meals and so on,
till the Supreme Pontiff orders all the bells
in Rome to be rung in order to exorcise
the evil spirits by whom he is haunted. At
Constantinople they befool the Sultan with
magic tricks. Mephisto disguises himself in
the official robes of the Pope and persuades
the Sultan that he is Mahomet (another
cut at the Pope, as Antichrist), while
Faust installs himself in the Sultan's
palace and enjoys life and finally floats up

40

into the air and disappears. They then visit Egypt, India, Africa, and other places, including the Garden of Eden and Britain.

Britain is described (rightly perhaps) as 'very damp—abounding in water and in metals. . . .' 'Here also is to be found,' adds our chronicler, 'the stone of God, which Doctor Faustus brought thence.' What he means by the stone of God is, I suppose, the so-called Philosopher's stone—used for the manufacture of money out of any worthless substance. Faust might have found a good deal of this stone of God without leaving Germany and seems to have left a considerable amount of it behind in Britain.

Part III of the Faust-book relates his 'feats of nigromancy at the courts of Potentates' and elsewhere, and his 'terrible end and departure.' At Innsbruck, in the presence of Charles V. and his court he summons up the shades of Alexander the Great and his consort, I suppose Roxana, the beautiful Bactrian princess. You may be interested to learn that Alexander the Great was a 'well-built stout little man with a thick yellow-red beard, red cheeks, and eyes like a basilisk,' and that the old chronicler, quite after the fashion of the modern purveyor for ladies' journals, informs us that Roxana wore a dress entirely of blue velvet trimmed with gold pieces and pearls.

The following chapters strike one as hardly in the same key with the rest of the book. They relate feats which remind one rather of Baron Münchhausen. Faust swallows up a wagon of hay and a team of horses that get in his way. He makes stag-antlers grow on the head of a nobleman—saws off his own foot to give it as security for a loan borrowed from a Jew (reminding one of Shylock and his 'pound of flesh')—treats students to wine magically procured (as in the scene in Auerbach's cellar in Goethe's poem)—cuts off people's heads and sends them to the barber to be shaved, and then replaces them (a most useful invention)—makes flowers appear in vases (like modern spiritualists or Indian jugglers)—and lets flowers and grapes flourish in his garden at Christmas-time. His most important feat is summoning up (as he does in Goethe's poem) the shade of Helen of Troy. You will wish for a description of Helen—at least of her dress. She appeared in a splendid robe of black-purple . . . her hair, of a glorious golden hue, hung down to her knees—she had coal-black eyes, a lovely face, and a round head, her lips red as cherries, with a little mouth and a neck like a white swan, cheeks red as a rosebud, and a tall straight figure.

A fit of remorse now seizes our magician. He is visited by a pious old man who nearly persuades him to repent and break his bond with the devil. But Mephisto is too cunning for him, and induces him to sign a new compact with his blood, promising to procure him Helen. For (as is also the case in Goethe's poem) Faust himself has fallen violently in love with the phantom that he had raised. By the help of Mephistopheles Helen herself—or one of her 'doubles' which play a part in Greek mythology—is summoned up, and lives with Faust as his wife. (At his death she, and their son, Justus Faust, disappear.)

In the last year he is overwhelmed with terrible despair, which is deepened by the mockeries of the demon. On the last evening he invites his friends to supper at the village Rimlich, near Wittenberg. After the supper he addresses his companions in a speech of intense and pathetic

43

remorse, praying that God will save his soul though his body is forfeit to the devil. He tells them that at the stroke of twelve the demon will come to fetch him. He begs them to go quietly to bed, and not to be alarmed if they hear a great uproar. At midnight a mighty wind sweeps over the house, and a terrible hissing is heard as of innumerable serpents. Faust's cries for help gradually die away. They rush into the supper room and find him torn to pieces —eyes, brains, and teeth scattered in all directions. 'After this,' says our chronicler, 'it was so uncanny in the house that no man dared live in it. Doctor Faust also appeared in person to his Famulus (assistant) Wagner by night, and related to him many still more weird and mysterious things. . . . And thus endeth the whole and truthful Historia and Magic of Dr. Faust, from which every Christian man should take warning, and specially those who are of a presumptuous, proud, curious and obstinate mind and head, that they may flee from all Magic, Incantation, and other works of the devil. Amen! This I wish for each and every one from the ground of my heart. Amen! Amen!'
44

AND GOETHE'S 'FAUST'

The great popularity of this original Faust-book led to the publication of many other versions of the story. In the very next year a Faust-book in rime appeared. In some of these versions Mephisto has a very bad time of it, Faust setting him all kinds of impossible tasks—such as writing the name of Christ or painting a crucifix, or taking him on Good Friday to Jerusalem—until the demon begs for his release, offering to give back the written compact. In Strassburg at a shooting competition Faust's magic bullet strikes Mephisto, who 'yells out again and again' in pain. In a Dutch version, where the demon has the name 'Jost,' Faust amuses himself by throwing a bushel of corn into a thorn hedge late at night, when poor 'Jost' is tired to death, and bids him pick up every grain in the same way as in the old story Venus vents her malice on Psyche. The most important German version was that by Widmann—an amplification of the old Faust-book. There also appeared a life of Faust's Famulus (assistant), Christopher Wagner, whom the devil attends in the form of an ape. Of one of these versions (I think Widmann's) there appeared about 1590 an English translation, which was

THE FAUST-LEGEND

supplemented by various English ballads on the same subject, and it was an Englishman —Shakespeare's great contemporary, the poet Christopher Marlowe—who was himself, as you know, a man of Faust-like temperament, and not unlike him in his fate —being killed in a drunken brawl—who first *dramatized* the story. His brilliant and lurid play, ' The Tragical History of Dr. Faustus ' follows very closely most of the details given in the German Faust-books. Its poetical beauties (and they are many) are unfortunately, as Hallam rightly remarks, intermingled with a great deal of coarse buffoonery. Possibly he had to consult the taste of his public in introducing such a large ingredient of this buffoon element—taken from what I called the Münchhausen portion of the old legend. Patriotic German commentators sometimes deny that Goethe knew Marlowe's play (though he knew Shakespeare well), but I think there is no doubt that the opening monologue of Marlowe's play inspired the more famous, though scarcely finer, opening scene of Goethe's drama. ' Theology, adieu ! ' Faustus exclaims, taking up a book of magic—

AND GOETHE'S 'FAUST'

These metaphysics of magicians,
And necromantic books are heavenly . . .
All things that move between the quiet poles
Shall be at my command—Emperors and kings
Are but obey'd in their several provinces,   *. .*
But his dominion that excels in this
Stretcheth as far as doth the mind of man.
A sound magician is a mighty god.
Here, Faustus, tire thy brains to gain a deity.

His agony of despair at the last moment
is very finely depicted, and there are not a
few passages in the play which, for beauty of
expression and thought, are truly Shake-
spearean. Some of you possibly know the
magnificent lines addressed to Helen of
Troy, which begin thus :

Was this the face that launched a thousand ships,
And burnt the topless towers of Ilium—

and the lines which seem to allude to the
identification of Helen with Selene, the
Moon-goddess—

O thou art fairer than the evening air
Clad in the beauty of a thousand stars.
Brighter art thou than flaming Jupiter
When he appeared to hapless Semele ;
More lovely than the monarch of the sky,
In wanton Arethusa's azur'd arms.

Marlowe's play was written about 1590.
Now it is asserted that about this time

English travelling players visited Germany, and perhaps introduced there Marlowe's drama ; and possibly *this* was the beginning of the German ' puppet-plays ' on the subject of Faust.   I do not feel quite sure about it. Faust puppet-plays seem to have existed almost simultaneously with the old Faust-books, and there is even the trace of one *before* the oldest Faust-book ; at least in the archives of the University of Tübingen an entry has been unearthed in which in 1587 two students were condemned to the 'Karzer,' or ' Black hole,' for composing a ' Puppen-spiel ' on the subject of Dr. Faust.

In these Puppenspiele (puppet-shows) the comic element largely prevails and is kept up by the comic figure Kasperle, a buffoon or ' Hanswurst ' of the same character as the Italian Pulcinella, the progenitor of our English ' Punch.' As might be expected, these puppet-shows introduced a great many variations of the story, most of them a mixture of tragedy and comedy.   In one a raven brings the contract from the devil for Faust to sign. One of the conditions is that for twenty-four years Faust is not to *wash*, or comb his hair or cut his nails—like Struwwel-peter. When Faust attempts to embrace

48

Helen she turns into a snake—and when he is finally carried off by the demon, Kasperle gives (what Euripides is accused of sometimes giving) a comic turn to the tragic catastrophe by cracking jokes.

For about 150 years after Marlowe no attempt was made by any German writer to use the subject artistically. Indeed during this period Germany, devastated by the Thirty Years War and afterwards by French literary influence, produced no literature worthy of mention, and what writers it possessed were not such as would be likely to perceive the poetic material contained in a popular puppet-show.

But the legend had taken firm hold on the popular imagination and when Goethe was a boy (he was born in 1749) he saw a Faust-puppenspiel at Frankfurt, and afterwards at Strassburg, when he was a young man of about twenty. He was at this time evidently also familiar with the old *Faustbuch* itself, and it was then (about 1770) that he seems to have first conceived the idea of the drama which he sealed up as finished sixty years later (1831), a few months before his death.

Goethe's early manhood coincided with

that period in German thought and litera-
ture which is called the ' Sturm und Drang '
—that is the Storm and Stress—period.
The subject of Faust, the attraction of
which had for so long lain dormant, ap-
pealed powerfully to the adherents of this
new school, with their gospel of the divine
rights of the human heart and of genius,
with their wild passionate graspings after
omniscience, their Titanic heaven-storming
aspirations after the unattainable and in-
describable.   Lessing himself, though never
a genuine Sturm und Drang writer, began
a *Faust*, and when Goethe began his drama
a new *Faust*, it is said, was being announced
in almost every quarter of Germany.   Some-
one (I think it was Bayard Taylor) has
reckoned up *twenty-nine Fausts* that were
actually published in Germany while Goethe
was working at his.   Some one else (I think
Ludwig von Arnim) has said : ' Not enough
Fausts are yet written.   Every one should
write one.   There is as much room for
them as for straight lines in the circum-
ference of a circle '—which, as you know,
is conceived by geometricians to consist of
an infinite number of infinitely small straight
lines.

None of these twenty-nine *Fausts* are, as far as I know, of any value or interest except the unfinished play by Lessing, which, as it was written while Goethe was still a lad, and seems to have been only printed in fragments at some later date, can hardly come under Bayard Taylor's list. From these fragments it is clear that Lessing meant to save Faust's soul, if not his body. Toward the end of the last act, when the devils are triumphing over their apparent victory and the possession of Faust's body, a voice from heaven is heard : 'Triumph not! Ye have not won the battle over human nature and human knowledge. The Deity has not given to man the noblest impulses in order to bring him to eternal misery. What you imagine you possess is only a phantom.'

Although we cannot tell for certain how Lessing meant to solve the problem, I think it is almost certain that Faust was to work out his own salvation amidst error and sin much as Goethe's Faust does. Before attempting (as I shall do on other occasions) to give a description of the two parts of Goethe's poem—in attempting which I shall keep as closely as I can to the original and to

questions arising directly out of Goethe's
own words—it will be useful and interesting
to consider the most striking points in which
his *Faust* differs essentially from all its pre-
decessors, except perhaps Lessing's—and
Lessing, although he struck the new chord,
did not resolve it. But this is a subject
involving many and far-reaching questions,
which, if they are to be solved at all, are
not to be solved by theory and dogma. I
shall therefore endeavour to state the case
as simply and as objectively as possible,
avoiding metaphysical cobwebs and giving
the *ego* and *non-ego* a wide berth. I shall
content myself in most cases with merely
pointing out the doctrine apparently
preached by Goethe (reminding you now
and then that even his own seemingly
categorical dogmas were to him merely
temporary forms of thought) and shall prefer
to let much justify its existence as an
integral part of the living whole rather
than to expel the life by dissection and
to examine the dead parts through the
spectacles of a commentator.

In my next lecture, after a brief con-
sideration of these preliminary questions,
I shall try to describe the first Part of the

drama—a task of more than common diffi-
culty, for the story is familiar to many of
you, and a bare rehearsal of the action of
the play would prove wearisome, while any
attempt to communicate by means of trans-
lation the wonderful beauty and force of
Goethe's words is almost bound to prove a
failure.

In my third lecture I shall treat the second
Part of the play, the action of which is far
less generally known. It is not often read
and is seldom seen on the stage. Indeed it
was not written for the stage and does not
lend itself to ordinary dramatic and operatic
purposes, as the first Part does with its
Gretchen episode. It embraces too huge
a circle—a circle within which lie all the
possibilities of human life. It is a kind of
framework for all the tragedies and comedies
and epics and lyrics ever conceived, or con-
ceivable. What unity it has is not of the
stage or the dramatic Unities. But never-
theless on the stage it produces effects
which impress one with the sense of an
imaginative power of an extraordinary kind.

Many years ago, when it was being given
in the Dresden theatre, I saw it performed
four or five times and I remember noticing

the wonderful attraction that it had for minds of a certain class (and no very limited class), while for others it was just such an unintelligible farrago of wearisome 'Zeug' as Dante's *Paradiso* and Beethoven's *Ninth Symphony* are sometimes said to be.

I believe it is the fashion with certain critics (especially with those who have read it superficially) to speak of the Second Part of Goethe's *Faust*, as they do of *Paradise Regained*, with a certain superciliousness, as a superfluous excrescence, the artistically almost worthless product of a mind that had worked itself out and had exhausted its 'Idea.'

The truth is that the *first* Part is only the merest fragment, and although the subject of Faust is endless and can never be fully treated in any one work of art (the whole poem ' necessarily remaining a fragment,' as Goethe himself said), nevertheless the *second* Part does solve in one of many possible ways the problem left unsolved by the first half of the poem, namely the final attainment of peace and happiness by the human soul, and it is one of the noblest monuments of the human intellect existing in the literature of the world.

54

Indeed it is, I think, still more than this. It is not merely a monument of intellect but of poetic imagination, and I am much inclined to believe that the *Paradiso* of Dante and the Second Part of Goethe's *Faust* are perhaps two of the best, the most infallible, touchstones for discovering whether we really possess what Tennyson calls the 'poetic heart'—not a trumpery æsthetic imitation but the genuine article.

II

GOETHE'S 'FAUST'

PART I

WHEN Goethe wrote to Schiller announcing
his intention of once more taking up his
unfinished *Faust*, Schiller replied : ' My
head grows dizzy when I think of it. The
subject of Faust appears to supply such an
infinity of material. . . . I find no circle
large enough to contain it.' Goethe
answered : ' I expect to make my work at
this barbarous composition, this *Fratze* [*i.e.*
caricature, as he often called it]' less diffi-
cult than you imagine. I shall throw a sop
to exorbitant demands rather than try to
satisfy them. The whole will always remain
a fragment '—a fragment, perhaps we may
add, in the same sense as even the grandest
Gothic building may be said to be only a
part of the infinitely great ideal Gothic

structure which will never be seen on earth, whereas in the Parthenon we have, or rather the Athenians in the days of Pericles had, something final and complete, something which will tolerate no addition.

If Schiller's head grew dizzy at the thought of a Faust-drama, I fear that one who has no Schiller head on his shoulders may prove a poor guide among the precipices and ravines of Goethe's life-poem, where the path is often very steep and slippery. But I will do my best; and perhaps I had better treat our subject as I proposed. At first I shall point out a little more distinctly some of the characteristics which distinguish Goethe's drama from the earlier versions of the story. Then I shall try to guide you steadily and rapidly through the action of the first Part, offering whatever comment may seem useful, and now and then perhaps asking you to step aside from the track in order to get a peep over some of the afore-mentioned precipices.

As we have already seen, one great differ-ence between Goethe's *Faust* and many older versions of the story (including Mar-lowe's play, but excluding Lessing's frag-ment) is the fact that the sinner is saved.

57

THE FAUST-LEGEND

Shortly before his death, in 1832, Goethe wrote to Wilhelm v. Humboldt: 'Sixty years ago, when as a young man I first conceived the idea of my *Faust*, the whole plan of it lay clearly before me.' From the first therefore Goethe had conceived the second Part as integral to his poem. He knew that, if he were to write a *Faust* at all, Faust must be saved.

We have already arrived at the edge of one of those precipices of which I spoke—Faust must be saved. But what did Goethe mean, or, to ask a fairer question, what do we ourselves mean, by being *saved?* No formula of words seems able to provide us with a satisfactory answer. We can indeed use metaphors drawn from the universe of Time and Space—we can speak of 'another world' and of a 'future life' —but as soon as we attempt to conceive such existence *sub specie aeternitatis* our imagination fails: to use the metaphor of Socrates, we are dazzled by the insupportable radiance of the eternal and infinite, and seek to rest our eyes by turning them toward shadows, reflexions, images: we accept the beautiful image —the enigma (as St. Paul calls it) or

allegory—of a heaven in some far interspace
of world and world.

As a poet, and especially as a dramatic
poet, Goethe, if he treated the subject at
all, was compelled to accept some imagina-
tive conception of a future life, and he
could scarcely accept any other but that
which was in keeping with the old legend
—that heaven of angels and saints and
penitents which was the converse of the
legendary hell and its fiends. Whether
however he was justified by the principles
of true dramatic art in his attempt to
depict his imaginative conception and to
place on the stage a representation of
heaven may be doubted. Certainly the
effect of Goethe's picture, especially when
seen on the stage, is such that one cannot
but wish some other solution might have
been devised, and one feels as if one under-
stood better than before why it was that
Shakespeare's dramatic instinct allowed no
such lifting of the veil. You remember
the last words of the dying Hamlet: 'The
rest is silence.'

Thus far therefore we have come: by
Faust being saved it is meant that he es-
capes from the fiend and reaches heaven,

THE FAUST-LEGEND

reaches the ' higher spheres ' of existence, as Goethe expresses it.

But the mere fact of his being saved does not form the essential difference between this drama and earlier versions of the story. The point of real importance is that he is not saved in a downward course by the intervention of some *deus ex machina*, some orthodox counter-charm. His course is not downward. His yearnings are not for bodily ease and sensual enjoyment but for truth—truth, not to be attained by speculation or scientific research but by action and feeling—by struggling onward through error and sin, and by gaining purification and strength from trial and suffering and resistance to evil; so that evil itself is a means to his salvation and Mephistopheles an instrument of good. Rising on the stepping-stones of his dead self he finds at last a certain measure of peace and is in the end reunited to her whose earthly happiness he had indeed ruined but whose love his heart has never forgotten. Indeed it is her love that is allowed to guide him ever aright and to draw him up to higher spheres.

When we once realize this we also realize

60

how meaningless, or how indescribably less full of meaning, the poem would be without its second Part. And yet many, when they speak of Goethe's *Faust*, mean merely the first Part—or perhaps merely the little episode of Gretchen given in Gounod's opera.

I spoke of Goethe's gospel of self-salvation. Since doing so I have recalled to memory some words of his which may seem to refute me. In reference to the song of the angels at the end of the poem he wrote as follows : ' These verses contain the key of Faust's salvation : namely, in Faust himself an ever higher and purer aspiration, and from above eternal love coming to his help ; and they are in harmony with our religious conceptions, according to which we cannot attain to heaven by our own strength unless it is helped by divine grace.'

It is true that *after death* Faust's soul is saved from the demons and is carried up to heaven by God's angels, but Goethe's drama is mainly the drama of Faust's earthly life, and from the ' Prologue in Heaven,' where, as it seems, the Deity undertakes *not* to help him, but leaves him to fight the battle entirely in his own strength, until the last

moment of his earthly existence there is no
hint whatever, I think, of anything but self-
salvation. On no occasion does he show
the slightest sense of his own helplessness
or of dependence on God's mercy. As for
remorse, Goethe regarded it as a false
emotion and as unworthy of a man.
Although the perfect balance of his mind
and his respect for much that he could not
himself accept saved him from the almost
brutal insouciance of such a form of ex-
pression he would probably have agreed
with Walt Whitman, who tells us that
animals should serve us as an example
because 'they do not lie awake in the dark
and weep for their sins; they do not make
me sick discussing their duty to God.'

Let us however dismiss criticism and turn
to what Goethe as poet has given us—
perhaps the noblest picture that dramatic
art can give: that of a man striving onward
and upward in his own strength, con-
fronting (as Goethe says in reference to
Shakespeare's plays) the inexorable course
of the universe with the might of human
will. We might take as the Alpha and
Omega of *Faust* these two lines from the
poem:

AND GOETHE'S 'FAUST

> *Es irrt der Mensch so lang er strebt,*

and

> *Nur rastlos betätigt sich der Mann,*

the sense of which is that human nature must ever err as long as it strives, but that true manhood is incessant striving.

It is a noble picture—perhaps the noblest conceivable. You remember Browning's lines :

> *One who never turned his back but marched breast*
> > *forward,*
> *Never doubted clouds would break,*
> *Never dreamed, though right were worsted, wrong*
> > *would triumph,*
> *Held we fall to rise, are baffled to fight better,*
> > *Sleep to wake.*

It will have already become evident what abstruse and insoluble questions present themselves—rise, as it were, like ghosts of many an ancient creed, on every side, as soon as we have crossed the threshold of this great Mausoleum of human thought and imagination. There is the spectre of the great Mystery of existence—of Life and Death and Eternity ; and that of the Knowledge of Good and Evil ; and that of Evil itself—a phantom assuming at times such a visible and substantial shape and then dissolving into thin air as mere negation. And

63

this Mephistopheles—are we to regard him
as a self-existent genuine demon of a genuine
Hell, or as our own mind's shadow? Is he
something external, something that we can
avoid, something that we can put to flight
by resisting and get entirely free of—or has
each one of us signed with the blood of his
human nature a compact with some such
spiritual power, with the demonic element
within him, with that spirit of negation, of
cynicism, of cold unideal utilitarian worldly-
wisdom which mocks at faith and love and
every high and tender impulse—that part
of our nature which, when some poor
girl is sinking in the abyss, prompts us to
answer our heart's appeal with the sneer of
Mephistopheles: 'She isn't the first!'? Surely
we can well understand the scorn and
contempt which Faust feels for this demon
companion of his. 'What canst thou, poor
devil, give me?' he exclaims—'Was the
human spirit's aspiration Ever understood
by such as thou!'

The real action of the play begins with
the celebrated monologue of Faust. But
this is preceded by a *Dedication*, by the
Prelude in the theatre, and by the *Prologue in
Heaven*, added at various periods of Goethe's

life. The *Prelude* consists of a scene between a poet, a theatrical director and a 'comic person.' It is merely a clever skit in which Goethe has a hit at the public and those who supply it with so-called drama. It has no organic connexion with the play. The *Prologue in Heaven* begins with the songs of the three Archangels—sonorous verses of majestic harmony, like some grand overture by Bach or Handel. These verses are, I think, meant to intimate the great harmonious order and procession of the natural and moral universe, as Pythagoras intimated them by his 'Music of the Spheres'—those eternal laws against which man, that tiny microcosm, so vainly strives.

Mephistopheles now enters, as in the Book of Job Satan is described entering God's presence, and, just as it happens in the Bible, the Lord asks him if he knows Faust, and, as in the case of Job, it is God himself who not only allows but seems even to challenge the demon to try his powers, foretelling his failure although promising no help to Faust. 'It is left to thee,' says the Lord to Mephistopheles. 'Draw this aspiring spirit from his fountain-head and lead him downward on thy path, if thou canst gain

a hold upon him, and stand ashamed when
thou shalt have to confess that a good man
amidst his dim impulses is well conscious of
the right way.'

That which distinguishes this scene from
the similar scene in *Job* is its irreverence.
Indeed one might almost call it flippancy,
and few would deny that at times this
flippancy is painful to them. The only
excuse that I can find for it is that, rightly
or wrongly, Goethe meant us to be pained.
I believe that here Mephistopheles represents
especially that element in human nature
which is perhaps the meanest and most dis-
gusting of all, namely flippant and vulgar
irreverence, and although we may not agree
with John Wesley's definition of man as
' half brute, half devil,' most of us will
probably allow that a certain part of our
nature (that part which Mephistopheles
seems to represent) is capable of an irrever-
ence and a vulgarity of which the devil
himself might almost be ashamed.

The monologue with which the action of
the play begins strikes at once the new chord
and gives us the leading motive—one so
entirely different from that of the old legend
—so indescribably nobler than that which

AND GOETHE'S 'FAUST'

is given in the opening monologue of
Marlowe's play. But the old framework is
still there. Faust renounces book-learning
and betakes himself to magic.

> *I've studied now philosophy,*
> *Jurisprudence and medicine,*
> *And e'en, alas, theology*
> *From end to end with toil and teen,*
> *And here I stand with all my lore,*
> *Poor fool, no wiser than before.*
> *No dog would live thus any more !*
> *Therefore to magic I have turned,*
> *If that through spirit-word and power*
> *Many a secret may be learned*
> *That I may find the inner force*
> *Which binds the world and guides its course,*
> *Its germs and vital powers explore*
> *And peddle with worthless words no more.*

Disgusted with the useless quest after that
science which deals only with phenomena
and their material causes, he turns to magic,
as he does in the old legend ; but it is here no
diabolic medieval wizardry which shall enable
him to summon the devil, for, as we shall see,
Faust does not summon the devil ; Mephisto-
pheles comes to him uncalled. Goethe has
merely used this motive of magic to intimate
attainment of perfect knowledge of Nature
through the might of genius—that revelation

67

of the inner secrets of the universe which he himself, in what he calls the 'Titanic, heaven-storming' period of his life, believed to be attainable by human genius in communion with Nature.

'Nature and Genius' was the watchword of the followers of Rousseau and the apostles of the Sturm und Drang gospel—a return to and communion with Nature, such as Wordsworth preached and practised, and such as Byron also preached but did not practise. Only to the human spirit in full communion with the spirit of Nature, of which it is a part, are revealed her mysteries. All other means, as Faust tells us, are useless.

Mysterious even in the open day
Nature within her veil withdraws from view.
What to thy spirit she will not display
Cannot be wrenched from her with crowbar or with
  screw.

Faust turns from his dreary little world of books and charts and retorts and skeletons. He opens the window and gazes at the moon floating in her full glory through the heaven. His heart is filled with a yearning to be 'made one with Nature,' and in words which remind one of certain lines of Wordsworth he exclaims:

O might I on some mountain height,
Encircled in thy holy light,
With spirits hover round crags and caves,
O'er the meadows float on the moonlight's waves.

Then, turning from Nature, he casts once
more a look around his dreary cell:

Ah me, this dungeon still I see,
This drear accursèd masonry,
Where e'en the welcome daylight strains
But duskly through the painted panes,
Hemmed in by many a toppling heap
Of books worm-eaten, grey with dust,
Which to the vaultèd ceiling creep
Against the smoky paper thrust,
With glasses, boxes, round me stacked
And instruments together hurled,
Ancestral lumber stuffed and packed—
Such is my world!   And what a world ! . . .
Alas !   In living Nature's stead,
Where God his human creatures set,
In smoke and mould the fleshless dead
And bones of beasts surround me yet.

He takes up the book of the Mystic
astrologer Nostradamus and sees in it the
sign, or cipher, of the universe.   As he
gazes a wondrous vision reveals itself: the
mystic lines of the cipher seem to live and
move and to form one living whole ; and in
spirit he beholds the Powers of Nature

69

ascending and descending and reaching to
each other golden vessels filled with the
waters of life and wafting with their wings
blessing and harmony through the universe.

And yet from this vision he turns away
dissatisfied:

> *What wondrous vision! yet a vision only!*
> *Where shall I grasp thee, Nature infinite?*

And from this cipher of the material uni-
verse, this vision of inconceivable immensity
and infinite diversity, the human spirit which
is not content with the dead bones of science
and has entered into communion with Nature
cannot but turn away dissatisfied—and even
with despair.   Let me try to illustrate this
in a more matter-of-fact way.

The human mind discovers, let us say,
that the earth is not the centre of the
universe; that the sun is larger than the
' bottom of a cask,' as in the old legend Faust
discovered it to be; that there are other
worlds quite as large as ours ; that this earth
of ours is a good deal smaller than the sun
and actually revolves round it; that even
the sun itself is not the centre of the universe
but one of many suns—one of the countless
stars in that enormous starry wreath that

surrounds us, and which we call the Milky
Way. And we direct our telescopes to this
Milky Way and find that what we took for
nebula is for the most part an accumulation
of countless millions of suns, each perhaps
with its planets. Then, as we sweep the
sky with our glass, we discover numberless
little wreath-like spiral cloudlets, and find
that they also are just such wreaths of count-
less millions of suns and solar systems, and
that these seemingly tiny wreaths are re-
volving round some central body or system,
which itself must revolve round some other,
and that again round another . . . until
imagination fails. Is there, we ask, some
final centre of all? some unmoved source of
motion? Or is the material universe infinite?

Then we turn our gaze in another direction
and we find in the tiniest grain of sand
countless millions of molecules whose atoms
(or electrons), it is said, are in perpetual
motion, revolving like the stars. Are then
(we ask) the stars themselves nothing but
molecules? Is the whole material universe
nothing but some grain of sand on the shore
of the ocean of eternity?

We turn away dazzled, and we rest our
eyes, as Socrates was wont to say, on images.

on reflexions. We try to make the mystery intelligible, or at least to pacify the reason by throwing it some such sop as the theory that ' Size is only relative,' or that ' Space is only a mode of consciousness ' and therefore nothing real in itself. Or we lull the mind to sleep with imaginative metaphors and speak (as Plato did) of the Central Fire of Hestia, the Hearth and Home of the Universe, or we call that mysterious unmoved centre of all motion the Throne of God. Thus we try to lay the spectre of infinite Space.

Or consider Time instead of Space. In a single second how many waves of light are supposed to enter the eye ? About 500 billions I believe. And of these waves some 500 would not exceed the breadth of a hair. Now any being to whom these tiny waves were as slow as the ripples on a pond are to us would live our human life of three score years and ten in the hundredth part of *his* second, while a being on one of those great worlds of space revolving but once in long æons around its centre would live—if his life were measured as ours—millions of our years. Here again. in our dazzlement, we have recourse to

72

metaphor and theory : we lay the spectre of Time by explaining it away as merely a 'mode' and as therefore of no objective reality. In other words, dazed and outworn by the incomprehensible infinities of Time and Space we console ourselves with the theory that it is all a mere phenomenon, a projection of our own mind, and with Faust we exclaim

What wondrous vision! yet a vision only !

and in the words of a still greater master of magic than Faust himself we despairingly add that

like the baseless fabric of this vision,
The cloud-capped towers, the gorgeous palaces,
The solemn temples, the great globe itself,
Yea all that it inherit, shall dissolve
And, like this insubstantial pageant faded,
Leave not a rack behind. We are such stuff
As dreams are made of.

From the cipher of the vast material universe, the Macrocosm, we turn away, as Faust did, with unsatisfied yearnings. Whither then shall we turn ? Where shall we grasp Nature—not the empty vision, but the warm living form ? It is in our own

73

heart that we find a refuge from the infinities
of Space and Time—in that human heart
by which we live, in its tenderness, its joys,
its fears. Here, and here alone, we find
those ultimate facts of existence which need
no explanation, and which we accept just as
they are, without any questionings. Here
we find an infinite universe—no less infinite
than that of Space and Time—the universe
of feeling.

From the cipher of the Macrocosm Faust
turns to that of the Earth-spirit, the spirit of
human life and feeling. He is filled with a
sudden, passionate yearning to share in the
joys and the sorrows and the aspirations and
the strivings of humanity:

> *Thou, Spirit of the Earth, art nearer.*
> *I feel my powers loftier, clearer,*
> *I glow, as drunk with new-made wine;*
> *New strength I feel out in the world to dare,*
> *The woes of earth, the bliss of earth to bear,*
> *To fight my way, though storms around me lash,*
> *Nor know dismay amid the shipwreck's crash.*

He calls upon this Earth-spirit, the Spirit
of human life. He bends all the might of
his human will to draw him down from his
sphere. 'Come!' he exclaims. 'Thou
must! Thou must!—e'en should it cost

74

my life!' Enveloped in blinding flame the
Spirit of life appears. At the apparition
Faust cowers back terrified and turns his
face away. But it is only for the moment.
Stung by the contemptuous words of the
phantom he answers: 'Shall I yield to *thee*,
Spectre of flame? 'Tis I, 'tis Faust, thine
equal!' The human Mind claims equality
with the Spirit of earthly life. But the
phantom exclaims: 'Thou art akin to the
spirit that thou comprehendest—not to me!'
—and disappears. Faust has yet to learn
a lesson that the mind of man can never
learn of itself, the real nature and meaning
of human life. But he has beheld the
vision of life, he has received the baptism of
fire. Henceforth he is to fight his way
through the storms of life and passion—to
pass onward and upward and at last to rise
to 'higher spheres'; and amidst the fierce and
insidious assaults of flesh and devil we shall
see that he looks for strength and guidance
to this Spirit that appeared to him in the
blinding vision of living empyreal flame.

Scarcely has the Earth-spirit vanished
when, with a timid knock, there enters
Faust's *famulus*, or assistant, Wagner. He
has heard Faust's voice and from its excited

tones has concluded that he is practising declamation—reciting perhaps a Greek play. The poor amiable dryasdust literary and scientific worm-grubber, whose maxim of life is *Zwar weiss ich viel, doch möcht' ich Alles wissen* (I know indeed a good deal, but I want to know *Everything*), wishes to profit from a lesson in elocution. A scene follows in which the contrast is graphically depicted between this half lovable, half contemptible scientific bookworm and Faust's Titanic heaven-storming aspirations after absolute truth. When he is once more left alone, longing to face the mystery of life but crushed by the contempt of the Earth-spirit, Faust is seized by despair. He shrinks from encountering life with its delusive joys, its pitiless injustice and its arbitrary fate. He resolves to seek certainty —to solve the riddle of life by death. As he moves the cup of poison to his lips there comes floating through the air the chime of bells and, perhaps from some near chapel, the hymn of Easter morn:

Joy unto mortals! Christ is arisen!

He pauses. Memories of childhood sweep over him, and he yields to the sweet voices that call him back from the threshold of the unseen.

Sound on sweet hymns of heaven ! As gentle rain
My tears are falling. Earth hath me again.

Thus Faust escapes the cowardly act of suicide and gains new strength through the awakening, for a time at least, of the consciousness, which had slumbered within him since the unreasoning days of childhood, that there is that beyond life which alone makes life worth having.

The next scene shows us Faust already in contact with human nature, as represented by holiday crowds flocking out of the town into the woods and adjacent villages at Eastertide. Those who know Germany well will feel the art with which Goethe at once transports us into the midst of a Germanic Feiertag in springtime, with its bright sunlight, its throngs of townspeople streaming into the country —happy and merry without vulgar rowdyism ; the smugly dressed apprentice and the servant-girl in her Sonntagsputz ; the pert student and the demure Bürgermädchen with her new Easter hat and her voluminous-waisted Frau Mama ; the sedate schoolmaster or shopkeeper, leading his toddling child; sour-faced officials; grey-locked and spectacled professors and 'town-fathers' discussing the world's news or some local grievance—all flocking countryward, with some Waldhaus or Forsthaus Restaurant as their ultimate goal. And those who know Frankfurt will recognize the scene at once: up there above Sachsenhausen, on the road to the pine-woods and the Jägerhaus, from which one sees the whole city lying below one, with its great Dom and its medieval gates—the river Main gliding through its midst and glittering away westward toward the Rhine; and in the far background the Taunus range and the dark Feldberg.

Amidst this scene, externally still the more than middle-aged German professor (he must be fifty-seven or so) but with a heart full of newly wakened yearnings for human life with all its joys and passions, Faust wanders, trying to feel sympathy with all these multitudinous human beings, attracted perhaps here and there, but evidently for the most part repelled and discouraged. He has yet to learn that a love for and a knowledge of humanity, such as he

78

finally reaches, must begin with love for
and knowledge of *one* human heart.

As he and Wagner return toward the
city Faust gives vent to his pent-up feelings
—pours contempt on his own book-learning
and wasted life and expresses his yearnings
for Nature, and the longing of his spirit for
wings to fly away into the infinite:

> *For in each soul is born the rapture*
> *Of yearning upward, and away,*
> *When o'er our heads, lost in the azure,*
> *The lark sends down her thrilling lay,*
> *When over crags and pine-clad highlands*
> *The poising eagle slowly soars,*
> *And over plains and lakes and islands*
> *The crane sails by to other shores.*

Whereat Wagner exclaims:

> *I've had myself at times an odd caprice,*
> *But never yet such impulses as these.*
> *The woods and fields soon get intensely flat,*
> *And as for flight—I never longed for that!*

Poor dear Wagner, how well one seems to
know thee, with thy purblind spectacled
eyes peering into fusty books and parch-
ments, or bending over thy crucibles and
retorts! Truly a novel and interesting sight
it would be to see *thee* assuming wings. In

79

thy philosophy there is naught but dreams
of elixirs of life or homunculi. Thy highest
aspiration nowadays would be to find the
mechanical equivalent of thought—to prove
that Shakespeare's and Dante's imagination
was due only to a slightly abnormal move-
ment of brain-molecules — to find some
method of measuring faith, hope and charity
in foot-pounds and thine own genius in
electric volts. Thou wouldst live and die,
as other eminent scientists of these latter
days have done, in the certain hope and
faith of demonstrating irrefutably that this
curious phenomenon which we call ' life '
is nothing but the chemical action set
up by the carbonic acid and ammonia
of the protoplasm.

As they walk and talk there appears a
black dog ranging to and fro through a field,
as if on the track of game. Ever nearer and
nearer he circles, and in his wake, as it
appears to Faust, trails a flickering phos-
phorescent gleam. But Wagner ridicules
the idea as an optical delusion. *He* sees
nothing but an ordinary black poodle.
' Call him,' he says, ' and he'll come fawning
on you, or sit up and do his tricks, or jump
into the water after sticks.' The poodle

follows them—and makes himself at home by the stove in Faust's study.

Faust has thus, after his first contact with the outer world of humanity, returned once more to his cell—to the little world of his own thoughts and feelings. He finds himself once more amidst his piled-up books, his crucibles and retorts, his bones and skulls. He lights his lamp and feels the old familiar glow of intellectual satisfaction. *But the poodle is there.* Faust has brought home with him something that will now haunt him to the last moment of his life. There has been awakened in his nature the germ of that acorn (to use Goethe's metaphor with regard to Hamlet) that will soon strike root and shatter the vase in which it is planted.

At present he is almost unconscious of this new presence. He is buried in thought, and his thoughts lead him toward the question of Revelation. He is drawn to take up a Bible and turns, with a mind full of metaphysical curiosity, to the passage 'In the beginning was the λόγος—the Word.' More than once there comes from the poodle a growl of disapprobation. Faust threatens to turn him out, and proceeds with his biblical criticism. . . . 'In the beginning was the λόγος.' How shall he translate λόγος? It cannot mean merely a 'word.' . . . A word must have meaning, *thought*—and thought is nothing without *act*. . . . So this 'Word,' this 'Logos,' must be translated as Act or Deed.

These speculations are interrupted by horrible growlings, barks, and howlings. As Faust looks towards the poodle he sees it rapidly swelling up into a monstrous form huger than an elephant or hippopotamus, with fiery eyes and enormous tusks in its gaping mouth. He tries to exorcise the phantom with 'Solomon's key' and other magic formulæ, and at length, when he threatens it with the mystic formula of the Trinity, it dissolves into mist, and out of the mist steps forth Mephistopheles, dressed as a 'travelling scholar'—an itinerant professor, or quack doctor.

I find that some commentators accuse Goethe of dramatic inconsistency and of interrupting the sequence of the action, because he makes Faust for a time return to his old speculations, and because Mephistopheles does not at once appear in the shape with which we are so familiar with his 'red gold-trimmed dress and mantle of stiff silk

82

and the cock-feathers in his hat,' the type of the dissolute man-about-town of the period. To me it seems very natural that, dispirited by his first contact with the outer world— unable to feel any real sympathy with the rollicking and sleek self-sufficiency of that holiday crowd, Faust should turn again to reflexion and speculation, and that when he is in this depressed and metaphysical mood the demonic element in his nature should first present itself—and that too in the disguise of an itinerant professor. For is it not the case that to many of us the devil *has* come first just at such a time and in just such disguise ?

Questioned as to his name and personality, Mephisto defines himself (he too being in a metaphysical mood) as 'the spirit of negation,' and as 'a part of that power which always wills evil and always works good '—' a part of that darkness which alone existed before the creation of light'—and he expresses the hope that, as light is dependent for its existence on the material world, both it and the world will ere long return to chaos and darkness. I have already touched upon this question of Evil as merely negative—merely a part of the whole—and will not detain you further over it.

THE FAUST-LEGEND

Mephistopheles now wishes to take his
leave, promising to visit Faust again. ‘Visit
me as you like,’ says Faust, ‘and now—there is
the window! there's the door! or the chim-
ney is at your service.’ But the devil must go
out by the same way as he has entered, and on
the threshold to keep out evil spirits Faust has
painted a mystic pentagram, a figure with five
points, the outer angle of which, being inaccu-
rately drawn, had left a gap through which
Mephisto had slipped in ; but being once in,
as in a mouse-trap, he cannot get out again.

As Faust now seems inclined to keep him
prisoner, Mephistopheles summons spirits,
who sing Faust to sleep. Then he calls a rat
to gnaw a gap in the pentagram, and escapes.

When, in the next scene, Mephistopheles
again appears, Faust is in a very different
state of mind, and Mephistopheles is also in a
different shape. He is decked out with silken
mantle and with cock-feathers in his hat,
ready for any devilry. Faust is in the depths
of morbid despair and bitterness at the
thought of life :

  ‘ *What from the world have I to gain ?—*
  Thou must renounce ! renounce ! refrain !
  Such is the everlasting song
  That fills our ears our whole life long . . .

84

AND GOETHE'S 'FAUST'

With horror day by day I wake
And weeping watch the morning break
To think that each returning sun
Shall see fulfilled no wish of mine—not one.'

He vows he would rather die. 'And yet,' sarcastically remarks Mephisto, 'some one a night or two ago did not drink a certain brown liquid.' Stung by the sarcasm, Faust breaks out into curses against life, against love and hope, and faith . . . and 'cursed be patience most of all!'

Here is the devil's opportunity. 'Life is yours yet, and all its pleasures. Of what's beyond you nothing know. Give up all this morbid thinking, these dreams and self-delusions! Be a man! Enjoy life! Plunge into pleasures of the senses! I will be your guide and show you the life worth living!'

In an ecstasy of embitterment and despair, though fully conscious that such a life can never bring him satisfaction and happiness, Faust exclaims: 'What wilt *thou*, poor devil, give me? Was the human spirit, in its aspirations, ever understood by such as *thou*? . . . And yet—hast thou the food that never satiates —hast thou red gold—hast thou love,

85

passionate faithless love — hast thou the
fruits that rot before one plucks them
—hast thou the fruits of that tree of
sensual pleasure which daily puts forth new
blossoms—then done ! I accept.' 'But if,'
he adds (and, alas, I must give merely the
sense of these noble verses—for all transla-
tion is so unutterably flat)—'if I ever lay
myself on the bed of idle self-content, if
ever thou canst fool me with these
phantoms of the senses, if ever I say to the
passing moment, *Stay; thou art so fair !*
—then let my life be ended. This wager I
offer thee.' 'Topp !' ('Done !') exclaims
Mephistopheles ; and, as you know, the com-
pact is signed by Faust with his own blood.

You will observe that here there is no
mention, as in the old legend, of any term
of years—the compact is *for life*. Of what
may come after this life Faust makes no
mention in his wager. He expressly says
that all he cares about, all he can know, is
this life, and that he will hear nothing about
any future life. This may be agnosticism
or whatever else we like to call it, but it is
not formally selling one's soul, with or
without one's body, for a *future* life and
for all eternity.

AND GOETHE'S 'FAUST'

Moreover Faust has *not* summoned the devil. The devil has come to him—is indeed a part of him. He does *not* league himself with a hell-fiend for the sake of worldly power or fame or sensual enjoyment, of which he speaks with contempt. He only offers to come forward into the battle of life and of passions to test the nobler powers and the deeper beliefs and the yet dim aspirations of his better nature against the powers of evil, against what he calls the 'cold devil's-fist' of negation and cynicism and disbelief, against the brute within the man.

> *Thou hearest me ! I do not speak of joy—*
> *I dedicate myself to passion --pleasure - pain —*
> *Enamour'd hate, and rapture of disdain.*
> *What's highest or what's lowest I will know,*
> *And heap upon my bosom weal and woe.*

Footsteps are now heard approaching. It is one of Faust's scholars. Faust 'has no heart to meet him'—and no wonder. He goes; and Mephistopheles, throwing around him Faust's professorial mantle and placing the professorial cap upon his head, awaits the scholar. The scene which ensues, in which Mephisto gives the young aspirant

87

for knowledge his diabolic advice and his diabolic views on **Science, Logic, Meta-physics, Medicine** and even **Theology**— would offer ample material for a very long course of lectures ; but as it is one which is not closely connected with the main action of the play it will have to be omitted. The scholar retires—his poor young head whirling round like a mill-wheel with the advice he has received and carrying away his album, in which the devil has inscribed his favourite text 'Ye shall be as gods, knowing good and evil.' Then Faust re-enters, Mephistopheles spreads out his silken cape, and on it the two fly away through the air on their adventures—first through the small and then the greater world—first the world of personal feelings and passions, then the greater world (is it really greater ?) of art and politics and Humanity.

Faust had said, as you remember,

What wilt thou, poor devil, give me ?
Was the human spirit in its aspirations
Ever understood by such as thou ?

This is the leading motive of all that follows. With ever-deepening disgust and contempt Faust, in his quest for truth through the jungles and quagmires of human passions, follows his guide. If ever Faust seems to catch sight of any far-off vision of eternal truth and beauty—as he does at times in his love for Gretchen, and again in his passion for ideal beauty in Helen, and once again in that devotion to the cause of Humanity which finally allows him to express a satisfaction in life, and thus causes his life to end—if ever Faust shows any sign of real interest or satisfaction, it is just *then* that Mephistopheles displays most clearly his utter inability to understand the 'human spirit in its aspirations'; and it is *then* that he shows most plainly his own diabolic nature, pouring out his cynical contempt and gnashing his teeth at what he deems Faust's irrational disgust for all those bestialities that seem to him (Mephistopheles) the sweetest joys of existence.

His very first attempt is a dead failure. He has carried Faust off through the air to Leipzig, and here he brings him into what to the Mephisto-nature doubtless seems highly desirable and entertaining company —to the 'sing-song' (as I believe it is called in England) of tippling brawling students. The scene is Auerbach's Cellar, a well-known Leipzig 'Kneipe'—a kind of Wine taproom or Bodega. Among these brawling comic-songsters Mephistopheles is in his element, and he treats them to a comic ditty :

Of old there lived a king,
  Who had a great big flea
As dear as any thing,
  Or any son, could be . . .

and so on. We need not linger over the repulsive scene—so graphically described.

Finally Mephistopheles bores holes in the table and draws wine from them.

The students come to handicuffs over it; they spill the wine, and it turns into flame.

Amidst their drunken uproar Faust and Mephistopheles disappear.

During the whole of this scene Faust *speaks no single word*, except a curt but polite greeting on entering the Cellar and an appeal to Mephistopheles to take him away from this 'scene of swinish bestiality.' How different from the part that Faust plays in the old story where he himself, not Mephistopheles, joins in the revelry and buffoonery !

90

Auerbach's Cellar existed till lately, though the house above it had been rebuilt. It was the original ' Keller ' that is mentioned in the old legend. In it were to be seen two old pictures (with the date 1525). One represented Faust sitting at table with students ; in the other he is flying off through the door astride on a wine cask.

A weird scene now ensues : the Witches' Kitchen.

Faust had asked how it was possible for him, the thought-worn grey-haired professor, to care for, or take part in, what Mephistopheles looked upon as ' life.' Mephistopheles therefore takes him to a witch, from whom he is to receive a magic draught that will ' strip off some thirty years from his body,' so that he becomes a young man of, say, about twenty-seven. This scene in the Witches' Kitchen is sometimes said to represent allegorically a long course of dissipation through which Mephistopheles takes Faust, and which of course could not be represented otherwise without extending the action of the play beyond all reasonable limits. It is true that after the draught Faust's character seems considerably changed for the worse. He develops a recklessness and a licentiousness which scandalize even Mephistopheles himself, who tells him that he is ' almost as bad as a Frenchman.'

Whether we should understand it thus, or not, I do not feel quite sure, but anyhow we have in future—to the end of the first Part—to take into account the fact that, although loathing all such swinish sensuality as that of tippling students, and hating all forms of mean selfishness and cunning and hypocrisy, Faust is (as so often is the case with otherwise noble and lovable men) open to assault at that point where, as nowhere else, the sensuous and ideal in our human nature seem to touch and coalesce.

When they enter the Witch is not at home. In the midst of the kitchen is a large cauldron, and at its side, skimming it and seeing that it does not run over is a Meerkatze—a kind of female ape. The Meerkater, or male ape, squats by the fire, warming himself, and near by are several young apes. Mephistopheles is enraptured at the sight of the ' tender pretty beasts,' but Faust finds them more disgusting than anything he has ever seen.

The apes perform all kinds of antics and

chatter a weird medley of half sense, half nonsense, in which one can dimly discern satirical allusions to various forms of the literary, political, and religious cant of Goethe's generation.

The animals enthrone Mephistopheles in a chair, give him a feather brush for a sceptre, and offer him a broken crown, which he is to glue together with ' sweat and blood.' It is like some horrid nightmare. We feel as if we were going mad ; and so does Faust himself. But suddenly he catches sight of a magic mirror, in which he sees a form of ravishing beauty—not that of Gretchen or Helen, but some form of ideal loveliness. He stands there entranced.

But at this moment the cauldron boils over. A great flame shoots up the chimney. With a scream the witch comes clattering down, and launches curses at the intruders— not recognising the devil in his costume as modern roué. He abuses her roundly and tells her that his horns tail and cloven hoof are gone out of fashion, modern culture having tabooed them ; and he forbids her to address him as Satan. That name is not up-to-date : he is now ' der Herr Baron.'

With a hocus-pocus of incantations she

brews the magic draught, which Faust drinks.
He is then hurried away by Mephistopheles
back into the world of humanity.

We have now come to the story of Mar-
garete or Gretchen, which by many, perhaps
by most, is looked upon as constituting the
main subject of Goethe's *Faust*. It is doubt-
less the part which attracts one, which appeals
to one's *heart*, more than any other, and it
forms by itself a pathetic little tragedy. The
story itself is merely the old sad story of
passion, weakness and misery, which has
been told thousands of times in all ages and
all languages.

It would be worse than useless to endea-
vour by any dissecting process to discover
how by some act of creative power Goethe
has inspired this little story with such
wondrous vitality that there is probably in
all literature scarcely any character that lives
for us, that seems so real, as Gretchen.
Possibly to feel this one needs a knowledge
of the original poem and an acquaintance
not only with that Germany which is
generally known to the English visitor, but
also with just that class of which Gretchen
is typical, and with just those little ways
and those forms of expression which are

peculiar to that class and to the part of Germany to which Gretchen belonged. Every single word that she utters is so absolutely true to nature that we seem to hear the voice of some real living Gretchen, and can hardly believe that she merely exists in our imagination. This may perhaps be asserted of other poetic creations; but I confess that I know no other, not even in Shakespeare, that produces on me quite the same kind of illusion. Homer's Nausicaa, the Antigone and Electra of Sophocles, Rosalind, Miranda, Imogen, Portia, Cordelia—all these live for me, but not quite as Gretchen. Their presence I feel as something living, but a little visionary. Gretchen I can see, and hear and almost touch. I need not recount at length her story, for it is too well known. I need only recall to you memories of certain facts and scenes: that first meeting in the street; the mysterious presents from the unknown lover; the meeting in the neighbour's garden and Gretchen's innocent prattlings about her home life; Faust's growing passion, and the vain battlings of his higher nature; the insidious promptings and cynical ridicule of his demonic companion; the song of Gretchen at her spinning-wheel; her loving

THE FAUST-LEGEND

anxiety as to Faust's religious opinions, and
his celebrated confession of faith ; the sleep-
ing draught by which Gretchen causes the
death of her mother; her shame, remorse
and despair; Gretchen kneeling with her
gift of tear-sprent flowers before the Virgin's
image ; the return of her brother, the young
soldier, Valentin, and *his* death—stabbed by
her lover (or rather by Mephisto) at night
beneath her window, and cursing her as he
dies; the scene in the Cathedral ; the pealing
organ and the solemn tones of the Dies Irae
mingling with the terrible words of the
accusing spirit, till Gretchen sinks fainting to
the ground.

And where is Faust? He has fled. The
avengers of blood are on his track. His selfish
passion has been the cause of death to
Gretchen's mother and brother and has
brought ruin on her—to end in madness,
infanticide and the block.

I have often wondered whether the limita-
tions of art might not allow the possibility of
some drama on the same lines as *Faust* in
which he might be saved by the purity and
nobility of womanhood, as in the story of
Cyprian and Justina, instead of, as here,
using the ruin of a poor girl as a stepping-

stone in his career of self-salvation. Or, what if he had felt such horror and remorse at her fate that he had broken his compact and freed himself from the demon? It will be said, perhaps, that this would have been undramatic and that such a view is merely sentimental and subversive of all true art. But, once more, what if he had bravely stood by Gretchen, or had even shared her fate when she refused to be saved by him?

Anyhow, Goethe did not choose any of these methods; and if he had done so we should have had no second Part of *Faust*— nor indeed our next scene, the *Walpurgisnacht*.

Pursued not only by the avengers of blood but by the avenging furies of his own conscience, Faust has plunged into a reckless life and experiences those after-dreams of intellectual and æsthetic extravagance which so often follow such riotous living. This period—that of sensual riot and æsthetic dalliance—Goethe has, I think, symbolized by two wild and curious scenes, the *Walpurgisnacht* and Oberon's Wedding, a kind of 'after-dream' of the *Walpurgisnacht*.

The connexion of these scenes with the main action of the play has puzzled many critics, especially the curious Intermezzo which follows the *Walpurgisnacht*, the 'Golden Wedding of Oberon and Titania,' a kind of dream-vision, or rather nightmare, in which besides the fairies of Shakespeare's fairyland, besides will-o'-the-wisps and weather-cocks and shooting stars, numerous authors, philosophers and artists and other characters appear, including Goethe himself as the 'Welt-kind.' This scene was not originally written for *Faust*, but Goethe inserted it (I imagine) as an allegorical picture of over-indulgence in æstheticism and intellectualism (the 'opiate of the brain,' as Tennyson calls it)—a vice into which one is apt to be seduced by the hope of deadening pain of heart. Although not written for the play, this Intermezzo cannot be said to be superfluous, for the subject of *Faust* is one that admits of almost any imaginative conception that is descriptive of the experiences of human nature in its quest of truth.

But let us return to the *Walpurgisnacht*. On the 1st of May a great festival was held by the ancient Druids, who on the preceding night used to perform on the mountains their terrible sacrifices, setting ablaze huge wicker-work figures filled with human beings.

98

AND GOETHE'S 'FAUST'

Hence in later times the superstition arose
that on this night witches ghouls and fiends
held their revels on the Brocken, or Blocks-
berg, in the Harz mountains. The name of
Saint Walpurga (an English nun, who came
to Germany in the eighth century) became
associated with this Witches' Sabbath, as the
1st of May was sacred to her. To this mid-
night orgy of the *Walpurgisnacht* Mephisto-
pheles takes Faust. . . . They are lighted on
their toilsome ascent of the Blocksberg by a
will-o'-the-wisp. A vast multitude of witches
and goblins are flocking to the summit ; the
midnight air resounds with their shrieks and
jabberings ; weird lights flash from every
quarter, revealing thronging swarms of
ghoulish shapes and dancing Hexen. The
trees themselves are dancing. The moun-
tains nod. The crags jut forth long snouts
which snort and blow. Amid the crush and
confusion Faust has to cling fast to his guide.
Once the two get parted, and Mephistopheles
is in anxiety lest he should lose Faust en-
tirely, the idea being, I suppose, that some-
times a human being outruns the devil
himself in the orgies of sensuality. At last
they reach the dancers. Mephistopheles is
here in his element and joins in the dances

with eagerness, bandying jokes with the old hags and flirting with the younger witches. Nor does Faust seem at all disinclined to follow suit. He however desists dismayed when, as he is dancing with a witch of seductive loveliness, a red mouse jumps out of her mouth.

At length, when Mephisto, who finds it getting too hot even for him, comes again to Faust, he discovers him silently gazing at a weird sight—one that might well have sobered him. 'Look!' says Faust:

' Look ! seest thou not in the far distance there,
Standing alone, that child, so pale and fair ?
She seems to move so slowly, and with pain,
As if her feet were fettered by a chain.
I must confess, I almost seem to trace
My poor good Gretchen in her form and face.'

Mephistopheles answers :

' Let her alone ! It's dangerous to look.
It's a mere lifeless ghoul, a spectre-spook.
Such bogeys to encounter is not good ;
Their rigid stare freezes one's very blood,
And one is often almost turned to stone.
Medusa's head, methinks, to thee is known !'

But Faust will not be convinced. It *is* Gretchen—his ' poor good Gretchen ' as he calls her. And what is that red bleeding gash around her neck? What terrible thought does it suggest!

> *'How strange that round her lovely neck,*
> *That narrow band of red is laid*
> *No broader than a knife's keen blade!'*

'Quite right!' answers Mephistopheles with a ghastly joke—

> *'Quite right! I plainly see it's so.*
> *Perseus cut off her head, you know.*
> *She often carries it beneath her arm.'*

He hurries Faust away. But soon these terrible presentiments are realized. Faust learns—how we are not told—that Gretchen is in prison, and condemned to death on the scaffold; for in her madness—yes, surely in madness—she has drowned her own child.

Instead of attempting to describe what follows, I shall offer a literal prose translation of some parts of the concluding scene, asking you to supply by your imagination, as best you may, the power and harmony of Goethe's wonderful verse.

A gloomy day. Open country.

FAUST *and* MEPHISTOPHELES. FAUST *is speaking.*

FAUST. In misery! In despair! Piteously wandering day after day o'er the face of the

101

earth,—and now imprisoned! That sweet unhappy being shut up in a dungeon, as a criminal, and exposed to horrible torments! Has it come to *this!*—to this! . . . Treacherous, villainous spirit! and *this* thou hast concealed from me! . . . Stand there, stand, and roll thy devilish eyes in fury! Imprisoned! In hopeless misery! Delivered over to evil spirits and the heartless verdict of mankind! . . . And *thou* meantime hast lulled me with loathsome dissipation . . . thou hast hidden from me her ever-deepening despair, and hast suffered her to perish helplessly.

MEPH. She isn't the first.

FAUST. Dog! Abominable monster! Turn him, O Infinite Spirit, turn this reptile back into his dog-shape . . . that he may crawl on his belly before me . . . that I may trample the abandoned wretch underfoot. Not the first! . . . Woe! Woe not to be grasped by any human soul, that *more* than *one* should sink into this abyss of misery—that the *first*, in her writhing agony before the eyes of the All-merciful, should not have made satisfaction for the guilt of all others. The misery of this *one* pierces with agony my deepest soul—and *thou* calmly grinnest at the fate of thousands!

MEPH. Here we are again, at the end of our wits! —where the common sense of you mortals loses its hold and snaps. Why dost thou make fellowship with us, if thou canst not carry it through? Wilt thou fly, and art not secure from dizziness? Did we thrust ourselves upon thee, or thou thyself upon us?

FAUST. Gnash not thy ravening teeth at me! I

loathe thee! Mighty, glorious Spirit—thou who didst deign to appear to me, and knowest my heart and soul, why dost thou fetter me to this satellite of shame, who revels in evil and gluts himself on destruction?

MEPH. Hast thou done?

FAUST. Save her, or woe to thee! The most terrible curse on thee for thousands of years!

MEPH. I cannot loose the bonds of the avenger—cannot undo his bolts. *Save her!* . . . Who was it that ruined her . . . I or thou?

[FAUST *glares wildly round him.*

MEPH. Wilt thou grasp after a thunderbolt? 'Tis well that it was not given to you miserable mortals! . . .

FAUST. Take me to her! She *shall* be free! . . . Take me to her, I say, and liberate her!

MEPH. I will take thee to her—and do what I *can* do. Listen! Have I all power in heaven and on earth?—I will becloud the jailer's senses. Then do thou get possession of the keys, and lead her forth with human hand. I will keep watch.—The magic steeds will be at hand . . . I will carry you off. So much lies in my power.

Night. The open country. FAUST *and* MEPHISTO-PHELES *galloping past on black horses. They pass a group of witches busy round their cauldron. They reach the prison. Within is heard the voice of* GRETCHEN *singing an old plaintive ballad.* FAUST *listens:*

'She dreams not' (he says) 'that her loved one

103

is listening, and hears her chains rattle and the straw as it rustles.'

[*He unlocks the prison door and steps in.*

GRETCHEN (*crouching into her bed of straw*). Woe, woe—they are coming! Bitter death!

FAUST. Hush! hush! I am come to free thee.

GRETCHEN (*grovelling before him*). If thou art a man, O pity my distress!

FAUST. Thou wilt awaken the watchmen with thy cries. [*He seizes her chain to unlock it.*

GRETCHEN (*kneeling*). Who has given you, heads-man, this power over me? You have come for me already at midnight. Pity me, and let me live! Is to-morrow morning not soon enough? And I am still so young—and I must die! Fair was I too, and that was my ruin. Pity me! What harm have I ever done to thee! I never saw thee before in all my life.

FAUST. Can I endure this misery?

GRETCHEN. I am wholly in your power. But let me first suckle my child. I held it in my bosom all the night. They took it from me, to vex me, and *now* they say I've killed it. . . . And I shall never be happy any more!

FAUST (*kneels beside her*). He that loves thee kneels before thee.

GRETCHEN. O let us kneel and call upon the saints. But . . . ah! . . . Look! . . . Under those steps, under the threshold, hell is flaming. The Evil One is raging there so furiously. Listen, how he roars and thunders!

FAUST. Gretchen! Gretchen!

104

AND GOETHE'S 'FAUST'

GRETCHEN (*listening*). That was the voice of my friend! Where is he? I heard him call. . . . Right through the howling and uproar of hell, through the horrid laughter of the devils, I recognized that sweet loving tone.

FAUST. It is I.

GRETCHEN. Thou! . . . O say it once more! (*Clasping him.*) It is! it is he! Where is now all my pain? Where is the anguish of the dungeon and the chain?

FAUST. Come! Come with me!

GRETCHEN. O stay! . . . I am so happy at thy side. . . . What! not one kiss! . . . Ah, woe, thy lips are cold. Where is all thy love? Who has stolen it from me?

FAUST. Come! Follow! . . . Be courageous, loved one! Come with me!

GRETCHEN. Thou art loosening my chain. . . . Know'st thou, my friend, *whom* thou art releasing?

FAUST. Come, come! Night is already on the wane.

GRETCHEN. My mother I have killed. I have drowned my child. Was it not given to thee and to me? Yes, to thee too. . . . And thou art really here! Thou! I can scarce believe it. Give me thy hand—thy dear hand! *Ah,* but it is wet. Wipe it, wipe it! It looks like blood upon it. O God, what hast thou done! Put up thy sword, I beg thee! Put it away!

FAUST. Let the past be past. Thou art killing me.

GRETCHEN. No—*thou* must live! . . . I will tell thee about the graves that thou must provide—

105

to-morrow. Give mother the best place, and brother close to her—and me a little on one side . . . only not too far away. And lay the little one in my bosom. . . . No one else shall lie with me. To cling to thy side, that was once such sweet blissful joy . . . but I seem no longer able . . . as if I had to force myself, and as if thou didst thrust me back. . . . And yet it *is* thou, and thou look'st so kind and good.

FAUST. If thou feel'st that it is I, then come!

GRETCHEN. Out *there?*

FAUST. To freedom!

GRETCHEN. I dare not. For me there is no hope more. What is the use to flee? They are lurking after me. . . . It's so wretched to have to beg, and that too with a bad conscience. It's so wretched to wander about in strange lands . . . and they'll catch me all the same.

FAUST. I shall be with thee.

GRETCHEN. *Quick! Quick!* Save it! Save my child! . . . Onward! Right up that path alongside the stream . . . over the bridge . . . there! . . . into the wood. . . . There! to the left! there, where the plank lies—in the pond! Catch hold of it! Catch it! It's rising! . . . It's struggling! Save it! save it!

FAUST. Bethink thyself! One step and thou art free!

GRETCHEN. If only we were over that hill! . . . There's mother sitting there on a stone. (Ah! what was that, like an icy hand, grasping my hair?) . . . She sits and wags with her head—she does not

GRETCHEN. I am thine, Father—save me! Ye angels, holy cohorts, encamp around me and defend me! (*To* FAUST.) Heinrich, I shrink from thee in horror.

MEPH. She is judged.

VOICE FROM ABOVE. She is saved.

MEPH. *to* FAUST. Here! to me!

[*Disappears with* FAUST.

[A VOICE FROM WITHIN—*the voice of* GRETCHEN —*calls on the name of him she once loved—of him who has robbed her of happiness and life itself. Fainter and fainter it calls, then dies away into silence.*

108

III

GOETHE'S 'FAUST'

PART II

THE picture which Goethe has given us in
Faust is in its main outlines the picture of
Goethe's own life. The Faust of Part I is
the Goethe of early days—of the Sturm
und Drang period—the Goethe of *Werther's
Leiden*, of *Götz*, of *Prometheus*, of
Gretchen, Lotte, Annette, Friederike and
Lili; the Faust of the earlier scenes of
Part II is Goethe at the ducal court of
Weimar; the Faust of the *Helena* is
Goethe in Italy, Goethe at Bologna, stand-
ing in ecstatic veneration before what was
then believed to be Raphael's picture of
St. Agatha, or wandering through the Colos-
seum at Rome, or writing his *Iphigenie* on
the shores of the Lago di Garda; and the
Faust of the last act of all is Goethe

reconciled to life and finding a certain
measure of peace and happiness in his
home, in the sympathy of his good-natured
but unrefined wife and of others whom he
loved, as well as in his scientific and philo-
sophical studies—until he seals up the
MS. of his great poem and (to use his
own words) ' regards his life-work as ended
and rests in the contemplation of the past,'
and then, a few months later, passes away
from earth, murmuring as he dies ' More
light!'

It will be remembered that at the end of
Part I Faust is dragged away by Mephis-
topheles and leaves poor Gretchen to her
doom. The fatal axe has now fallen.
Gretchen is dead.

In the opening scene of Part II we find
him ' lying on a grassy bank, worn out
and attempting to sleep.' A considerable
time has evidently elapsed—a time doubt-
less of bitter grief and of the fiercest
accusation against his evil counsellor, that
part of his human nature which is repre-
sented by Mephistopheles and from which
even in the last hour of his life (as we shall
see) he confesses it to be impossible wholly
to free himself:

Dämonen, weiss ich, wird man schwerlich los.
Das geistig-strenge Band is nicht zu trennen.

'From demons it is, I know, scarce possible to free oneself. The spiritual bond is too strong to break.'

But it is not from grief or self-accusation that Faust is to gain new inspiration. It is from the healing power of Nature—in which Goethe believed far more than in remorse.

The scene amidst which Faust is now lying reminds one of some Swiss valley. The rising sun is pouring a flood of golden light over the snow-fields of the distant mountains and down from the edge of an overhanging precipice is falling a splendid cataract, such as the Reichenbach or the Staub-bach, amidst whose spray gradually forms itself, as the sunshine touches it, an iridescent bow, brightening and fading, but hanging there immovable. Through this scene are flitting elfin forms—Ariel and his fays—singing to the liquid tones of Aeolian harps and lapping Faust's world-worn senses in the sweet harmonies of Nature, tenderly effacing the memories of the past and inspiring him with new hopes and new strength to face once more the battle of life.

THE FAUST-LEGEND

He watches the rising sun, but blinded by excess of light he turns away, unable to gaze upon the flaming source of life, as erst he had turned from the apparition of the Earth-spirit. He seeks to rest his dazzled eyes in reflected light (a metaphor used, as you may remember, also by Socrates in the parable of the Cave)—in the sun-lit mountain slopes, the pine-woods and the glittering walls of rock, and in the colours of the foam-bow suspended amidst the spray of the swift down-thundering cataract. In the ever-changing colours but motionless* form of this bow hanging over the downward rush of the torrent Faust finds a symbol of human life suspended with its ever-varying hues above the stream of time.

It is one of the truest and the most beautiful of all similitudes, this of pure sunlight refracted and broken into colours, symbolizing the One and the Many, the perfect and the imperfect, the eternal and the temporal. Doubtless you are already thinking of Shelley's magnificent lines :

The One remains, the Many change and pass ;
Heaven's light for ever shines, Earth's shadows fly,
Life, like a dome of many-coloured glass,
Stains the white radiance of eternity.

112

Into such variegated scene of reflected and refracted light Faust is now entering. He has passed through the 'little world' of personal feeling—the world of the One, of the heart, and he is entering what Mephistopheles calls the 'greater world' (for greater it appears to be from the Mephistophelean standpoint)—the world of the 'many,' of politics and ethics and art and literature and society—the world whose highest ideal is success, or, at the best, the 'greatest good of the greatest number' and the evolution of that terrible ghoul the so-called Super-man.

It is at the court of a German Kaiser that Faust first makes trial of this so-called greater world. The young monarch has lately returned from Italy, where, as was once customary, he had been crowned by the Pope with the iron Lombard crown. By his extravagances he has already emptied the imperial coffers. His Chancellor, his Treasurers, his Paymasters are all at the verge of despair, and the Empire is on the brink of bankruptcy. To add to these misfortunes (perhaps the greatest of them in the opinion of the young Kaiser) the court-fool has tumbled downstairs and has broken his neck; so at least it is believed; but cats and fools have a way of falling on their feet, and this fool turns up again later. Meanwhile however Mephistopheles presents himself and is accepted as a *locum tenens*. To him the Kaiser turns for advice, and Mephistopheles proposes a clever expedient—meant as a satire on modern systems of finance and State security. He suggests that, as the land belongs to the Kaiser, and as in the ground there are doubtless great quantities of hidden treasures, buried in olden times, the Kaiser should, on the security of these hidden and as yet undiscovered treasures, issue 'promises to pay'—in other words paper money. This is done, and suddenly the imperial court, in spite of its empty coffers, finds itself in affluence. The young Kaiser, delighted at the opportunity of indulging his taste for display and extravagance, decides on holding a masquerade, such as he had lately witnessed at the Roman Carneval.

The description of this great court masquerade occupies a considerable space in Goethe's drama, and is generally looked upon by the commentators as one of the least

114

successful parts of *Faust*. The question is, how are we to estimate *success* in such a matter? For myself I confess that I find this masquerade scene tedious and irksome, and can with difficulty read it through; but is not this just the effect that Goethe wished to produce? Is not this just the effect that society, with all its masquerades and mummeries, inevitably produces on any one who, like Faust and with Faust's ideals and aspirations, is making trial of life in order to discover under what conditions it is worth living? Instead of telling us in so many words that Faust makes trial of all the pomps and vanities of fashionable society and finds them utterly empty and ridiculous, fatal to all true life and disgusting to all true manliness, Goethe gives us a picture of this tiresome foolish scene, with all its absurdities and falsities and trumpery grandeurs, amidst which our friend Mephistopheles is so entirely in his element, and where Faust, with evident self-contempt and disgust, forces himself for a moment to play a part. The various elements of fashionable society— and, as a contrast, certain very unfashionable elements—are introduced under the

disguise of these masked figures. Market-
able belles and heiresses in the guise of
flower-girls offer their charms and their
fortunes in the form of flowers and fruits to
the highest bidder. The anxious mother is
there with her daughters, hoping that
among so many fools *one* may be at last
secured. Idlers, parasites, toadies, club-
frequenters and diners-out are there in the
masks of court-fools, and buffoons. The
working man, the trade-unionist and the
striker, comes marching amidst this scene
of revelry, forcing his way through the
ranks of consternated society, roughly
asserting the sole nobility of labour and
demanding the overthrow of the aristocrat
and the capitalist—no new cry, as you see !
Indeed it is as old as Rome and Athens
and Babylon—as old, almost, as humanity
itself. Then appear the Graces, symbols of
the refinements and elegancies of life, and
the Fates, symbolizing the powers of Order
and Law, and the Furies, the types of revolu-
tion and war, and a huge elephant, the
incorporation of the unwieldy State or
Public, reminding one of the ' Levia-
than ' of the philosopher Hobbes, and
Thersites (that evil-tongued mischief-maker

described by Homer) representing society-scandal and calumny. Then comes a chariot whose charioteer is a beautiful boy, representing art or poetry. He is the same Euphorion whom we shall meet later as the son of Faust and Helen, and identical with Byron. On the chariot is enthroned Faust as Plutus the God of Money, and behind him as groom or armour-bearer sits Mephisto, an emaciated hollow-eyed apparition denoting Avarice. Nymphs, Fauns, Satyrs and Gnomes—types of the powers of Nature—attend the car and do homage to the God of Money. The gnomes offer to show their master Plutus a subterranean treasure-horde of molten gold. He approaches too close and his beard catches fire. In a few moments an immense conflagration spreads through the crowds of revellers, which would have ended in a terrible catastrophe (such as had actually happened at the French court shortly before Goethe wrote this scene, and such as happened some fifteen years ago in Paris at some bazaar) had not Faust with the help of Mephistopheles extinguished the flames by the aid of magic.

The young Kaiser now demands from

Faust that he shall give the court a display
of his magic arts. He commands him to
raise the shades of Paris and Helen.
Faust applies to Mephisto, but he professes
himself unable to raise the shades of
classical heroes and heroines. 'This heathen
Greek folk,' he says, 'have their own hell
and their own devils. *I* have no power
over them. Still — there *is* a means.'
He then tells Faust that he will have to
descend to the 'Mothers,' 'die Mütter,'
mysterious deities (mentioned by Greek
authors) as worshipped in Sicily and
dwelling in the inmost depths of the
universe, at the very heart of Nature,
beyond the conditions of Time and Space.
He who will raise the shade of Helen, or
ideal beauty, must descend first to the
'Mothers'—must enter the realm of the
spiritual, the unconditioned, the ideal, to
which there is no defined road, and to
which even *thought* cannot guide him. He
must surrender himself in *contemplation* and
sink to the very centre of the world of
appearances. Mephistopheles gives Faust a
key, which glows and emits flames as he
grasps it. Holding this key he will sink
down to the realm of the Mothers, where

he will find a glowing tripod (the symbol of
that Triad or Trinity which plays so large a
part in the old Pythagorean philosophy and
in more than one religion). This tripod he
is to touch with the key, and it will rise with
him to the surface of the earth.

The imperial court is assembled. A
stage has been erected. The court astro-
loger announces the play and Mephis-
topheles is installed in the prompter's box.
All is in expectation and excitement.
Then on the stage is seen rising from the
ground the form of Faust attended by the
tripod. He touches the tripod with the
glowing key. A dense mist of incense
arises, and as it clears away is seen—Paris.
His appearance is greeted by the enthu-
siastic comments of the court ladies, young
and old, and criticized by the men courtiers—
with evident jealousy. Helen then appears,
and the comments and criticisms are re-
versed, female jealousy now having its turn.
Faust stands entranced at the loveliness of
Helen. In spite of the angry protests of
Mephistopheles from the prompter's box,
who tells him to keep to his rôle and not to
be taken in by a mere phantom of his own
raising, Faust, unable any longer to con-

trol himself when Paris attempts to carry
off Helen, rushes forward to rescue her. A
great explosion takes place and all is
darkness. Faust has fallen senseless to the
ground. Mephistopheles picks him up
and carries him away—with contemptuous
remarks.

At the beginning of the next act we find
Faust lying, still insensible, on his bed in his
old room, where we first met him—his pro-
fessor's study. His daring attempt to grasp
ideal beauty has ended, as it often does end,
and as it ended in Goethe's own case, in
failure of a sudden and explosive nature. He
is now to have an experience of a different
nature. During the years while he has been
making his first trial of the outer world, his
old Famulus, Wagner, now professor in
Faust's place, has been devoting *his* whole
time and energies to realizing that dream of
science—the chemical production of life.

It is, says Professor Romanes, 'the dream
of modern science that a machine *may* finally
be constructed so elaborate in its multiple
play of forces that it would begin to show
evidences of consciousness and mind '—mind
and motion being, according to certain
modern scientists, identical. Curiously
120

enough a scientist of the same name—
Wagner—who lived in the last century, did,
like Faust's Famulus Wagner, in the same
way devote his life to the production of a
living organism—a 'homunculus'—in the
conviction, as he asserted, that 'in course of
time chemistry is bound to succeed in produc-
ing organic bodies and in creating a human
being by means of crystallization '—an asser-
tion not very different from that of a still more
trustworthy scientist, for Professor Huxley
himself has told us that he lived in ' the hope
and the faith that in course of time we shall
see our way from the constituents of the
protoplasm to its properties,' *i.e.* from
carbonic acid, water, and ammonia to that
mysterious thing which we call vitality or
life—from the molecular motion of the brain
to Socratic wisdom, Shakespearean genius,
and Christian faith, hope and charity.

In the background of the stage we see
Faust still lying insensible on his bed.
Mephistopheles comes forward muttering
sarcastic comments on Faust's foolish in-
fatuation. 'He whom Helen paralyzes,' he
says, ' doesn't come to his wits again so soon.'
He then pulls the bell. The windows rattle
and the walls shake, as with earthquake.

Wagner's terrified Famulus appears. He says that his master, the Herr Professor, has locked himself up for days and nights together in his laboratory; that he is engaged in a most delicate and important operation, namely that of manufacturing a human being, and he really cannot be disturbed. Mephistopheles however sends him back to demand admittance. Meanwhile he dons Faust's professorial costume, which he finds hanging in its old place but infested with legions of moths, which buzz around him piping welcome to their old mate. Then he takes his seat in Faust's professorial chair, and the same scholar enters to whom as a timid 'Fuchs,' or freshman, Mephistopheles had in the first Part of the play given his diabolic advice as to the choice of a profession. The scholar is *now*, after a course of University education, a match for the devil himself. He flouts poor Mephisto as a dried-up old pedant, not up to date with the new generation's æsthetic and literary self-conceits, or with its contempt for its elders—and for everything else except its own precious self. 'Youth and its genius,' he exclaims, 'are the only things of value; as soon as one is thirty years of age he's just as good as

122

AND GOETHE'S 'FAUST'

dead . . . and it would be far better if all people at thirty were knocked on the head'; and he storms out of the room. Mephistopheles consoles himself with the fact that the devil is old enough to have seen a good many such new generations, with all their absurdities, their up-to-date fads and follies, pass away and give place to other forms of still more up-to-date and self-conceited absurdity.

Mephisto now enters the laboratory, where Wagner is intently engaged in watching his chemical compound gradually crystallizing' within a huge glass retort. As he watches, the outlines of a diminutive human being—a mannikin or 'homunculus'—become visible and rapidly gain distinct form. A tiny voice is heard issuing from the glass retort and addressing Wagner as 'Daddy' and Mephistopheles as 'Cousin'; and it is to the presence of this 'Cousin,' we may infer, rather than to his scientific 'Daddy' that the Homunculus really owes his existence. With the connivance of Mephistopheles, the Mannikin, still in his glass retort, slips from the enamoured paternal grasp of Wagner, and floats through the air into the adjacent room, hovering above Faust, who is still asleep on his couch.

THE FAUST-LEGEND

As it hovers above the sleeper it begins to sing—to describe ravishing dreamland scenery—inspiring Faust with visions of sensuous loveliness. It then bids Mephistopheles wrap Faust in his magic mantle and prepare for an aerial flight. . . . 'Whither?' asks Mephistopheles. '*To Greece!*' is the answer: to the Pharsalian plain in Thessaly; and in spite of the protests of Mephistopheles (who has no taste for the land of classic art) he is forced to obey. The sleeping form of Faust is borne aloft, the Mannikin leading the way like a will-o'-the-wisp, gleaming within his glass retort. '*Und ich?*' exclaims poor old Wagner in piteous accents. '*Ach, du!*' says Homunculus, '*Du bleibst zu Hause—!*' 'You just stop at home, and grub away among your musty manuscripts, and work away at your protoplasms and your elixirs of life.' Thus, guided by the Homunculus, Faust and Mephistopheles set forth on their aerial journey to ancient Greece—to the land where the ideals of art have found their highest realization—in quest of Helen, the supreme type of all that the human mind has conceived as beautiful.

It is often asked, and I think *we* may fairly ask, what Goethe meant to symbolize

124

by his Homunculus. You will have noticed
that his material components (as the car-
bonic acid and ammonia of Professor
Huxley's protoplasm) are supplied by his
scientific 'Daddy,' but that the 'tertia vis,'
that third power or 'spiritual bond' which
combines his material components, is sup-
plied by the supernatural presence of
Mephistopheles. I believe this Homun-
culus to be a symbol of poetic genius or
imagination, which uses the material sup-
plied by plodding pedantry — by critical
research, antiquarianism, scholarship, and
science—slips from the hands of its poor
enamoured Daddy, and flies off to the land
of idealism. Here, as we shall see, the
Mannikin breaks free from his glass retort
and is poured out like phosphorescent light
on the waves of the great ocean.

But the quest for Helen, for ideal beauty,
leads through scenes haunted by forms of
weird •and terrible nature—those forms in
which the human imagination, as it gradually
gains a sense of the supernatural and a sense
of art, first incorporated its conceptions—
forms, first, of hideous and terrific character :
monstrous idols of Eastern and Egyptian
superstition, Griffins, and Sphinxes, and bull-

headed Molochs, and horned Astartes, and many-breasted Cybeles, till in the Hellenic race it rose to the recognition of the beautiful and bodied forth divinity in the human form divine, and found its highest ideal of beauty in Helen, divinely fair of women. This phase in Faust's development—this stage in his quest for beauty and truth—this delirium of his 'divine madness,' as Plato calls our ecstasy of yearning after ideal beauty, is symbolized by the classical *Walpurgisnacht.* (You remember the other *Walpurgisnacht*— that on the Blocksberg—which I described before.)

Guided by the Mannikin, Faust and Mephistopheles arrive at the Pharsalian fields—the great plain of Thessaly, renowned for the battle of Pharsalus, in which Caesar conquered Pompey—renowned too as the classic ground of witches and wizards. Griffins, Sphinxes and Sirens meet them. They can tell Faust nothing about Helen, but they direct him to Cheiron the Centaur (a link, as it were, between the monstrous forms of barbarous oriental imagination and Hellenic art). Cheiron the Centaur has himself borne Helen on his back, and excites Faust's passion by the

126

description of her beauty. He takes Faust
to the prophetess Manto, daughter of the
old blind Theban prophet Teiresias, and she
conducts him to a dark fissure—a Bocca
dell' Inferno—at the foot of Mount Olympus,
such as that which you may have seen in
the Sibyl's cave on Lake Avernus; and
here (as once Orpheus did in search of
Eurydice) he descends to the realms of the
dead to seek the help of Persephone, Queen
of Hades, in his quest for Helen. Mean-
while Mephisto has found that in spite of
his distaste for classic art and beauty there
are elements in the classical witches' sabbath
not less congenial to him than those of the
Blocksberg with its northern and more
modern types of devilry and bestiality.
He is enchanted with the ghoulish vampire
Empusa and the monster Lamia, half-snake
half-woman, and at length finds *his* ideal
of beauty in the loathsome and terrible
Phorkyads, daughters of Phorkys, an old
god of the sea. The Phorkyads are some-
times described as identical with, sometimes
as sisters of, the Gorgons, and represent the
climax of all that Greek imagination has
created of the horrible. The three sisters
are pictured in Greek mythology as pos-

127

sessing between them only one eye and one
tooth, which they pass round for use. They
dwelt in outer darkness, being too terrible
for sun or moon to look upon. Even
Mephistopheles is at first a little staggered
by the sight, but he soon finds himself on
familiar terms with them and ends by
borrowing the form of one of them (she
becoming for the time absorbed into her
two sisters)—for as medieval devil he has no
right of entrée into that classical scene in
which he and Faust are now to play their
parts. It is therefore in the form of a
Phorkyad or Gorgon that Mephisto will
appear when we next meet him.

Meanwhile the Homunculus has found
congenial spirits among the sea-nymphs and
sirens on the shores of the Aegean. He
longs to gain freedom from his glass, in
which he is still imprisoned. Nereus the
sea-god is unable to help him, but sends
him to his father Proteus, the great ocean
prophet, who bears him out into the midst
of the ocean. Here Galatea the sea-goddess
(identical with Aphrodite, the sea-born
symbol of the beauty of the natural world)
passes by in her chariot drawn by dolphins
and surrounded by Nereids. The Homun-
128

culus in an ecstasy of love dashes himself against her chariot. The glass is shattered and he is poured forth in a stream of phosphorescent light over the waves—thus being once more made one with Nature.

The theory that *water* was the prime element, a theory advocated especially by the old Ionic philosopher Thales, was held by Goethe, who was a 'sedimentarist' in geological matters, and in this classical *Walpurgisnacht* he has introduced, much to the annoyance of many critics, a dispute between Thales and other sages on the question whether the formation of the world was due to fire or water.

We have now reached that part of *Faust* which is known as the *Helena*. It was written before the rest of Part II, though doubtless when he wrote it Goethe had already conceived the general outline of the whole poem. Of the wonderful versatility of Goethe's genius no more striking example can be given than the sudden and complete change of scene, and not only scene but ideas and feelings, by which we are transported from the age of Luther and the court of a German Kaiser and the laboratory of a modern scientist back

—some 3500 years or so—to the age of the Trojan war.

Instead of extravagance and grotesqueness, instead of the diversity, the rich ornamentation, the heaven-soaring pinnacles and spires of Gothic imagination we have in the *Helena* sculpturesque repose, simplicity, dignity and proportion. It is as if we had been suddenly transported from some Gothic cathedral to the Parthenon, or to Paestum.

I know no poet who in any modern language has reproduced as Goethe has done in his *Iphigenie* and in the *Helena* not only the external form but also the spirit of Hellenic literature. While reading the *Helena* we feel ourselves under the cloudless Grecian sky; we breathe the Grecian air with Helen herself.

The scene is laid before the palace of Menelaus at Sparta. Helen, accompanied by a band of captive Trojan maidens, has been disembarked at the mouth of the river Eurotas by Menelaus, on his return from Troy, and has been sent forward to Sparta to make preparation for the arrival of her husband and his warriors. Once more after those long eventful years since she had fled to Troy with Paris she stands as in a dream before her own palace-home, dazed and wearied, her mind distraught with anxious thoughts; for during the long wearisome return across the Aegean sea her husband Menelaus has addressed no friendly word to her, but seemed gloomily revolving in his heart some deed of vengeance. She knows not if she is returning as queen, or as captive, doomed perhaps to the fate of a slave.

She enters the palace alone. After a few moments she reappears, horror-struck and scarce able to tell what she has seen. Crouching beside the central hearth she has found a terrible shape—a ghastly haggard thing, like some phantom of hell. It has followed her. It stands there before her on the threshold of her palace. In terrible accents this Gorgon-like monster denounces her, recounting all the ruin that by her fatal beauty she had wrought, interweaving into the story the various legends connected with her past life—those mysterious legends that connect Helen not only with Paris and Menelaus but with Theseus and Achilles and with Egypt — legends of a second phantom-Helen, the ' double of that Helen whom Menelaus has carried home from Troy—until alarmed and distracted, doubting her own identity, overwhelmed by anxiety about the future and by terror at the grisly apparition, she seems herself to be in truth fading away into a mere phantom, and sinks senseless to the ground. After a fierce altercation between the chorus of captive maidens and the Gorgon-shape (in whom you will have recognized our old friend Mephistopheles) Helen returns to consciousness. Then the Phorkyad-Mephistopheles tells her that the preparations which she has been ordered to make are in view of a sacrifice to be performed on the arrival of Menelaus and that she herself (Helen) is the destined victim.

In despair Helen appeals to the Gorgon for advice, who bids her take refuge in the neighbouring mountains of Arcadia, where a robber chieftain has his stronghold. Under the guidance of Mephisto, who raises a thick mist, she and her maidens escape. They climb the mountain; the mists rise and they find themselves before the castle of a medieval bandit-prince, and it is Faust himself who comes forth to greet her and to welcome her as his queen and mistress.

AND GOETHE'S 'FAUST'

Faust, the symbol of the Renaissance and modern art, welcomes to his castle the ideal of Greek art and beauty.

The stately Greek measures now give way to the love-songs of Chivalry and Romance—to the measures of the Minnesinger and the Troubadour. Faust kneels in homage before the impersonation of ideal beauty, and Helen feels that she is *now* no longer a mere ideal, a mere phantom. She clings to her new, unknown lover, as to one who will make her realize her own existence. It is an allegory of modern art—the art of Dante, Giotto, Raphael, Shakespeare and Goethe—receiving as its queen the ideal of Greek imagination and inspiring, as it were, the cold statue with the warm vitality of a higher conception of chivalrous love and perfect womanhood.

I have mentioned how the stately Greek measures in the *Helena* give way to the metres of Romance and Chivalry. Perhaps it may be well to explain some of these various metres.

The scene opens, as you know, with Helen's dignified and beautiful speech:

Bewundert viel und viel gescholten Helena.

That is the well-known *iambic trimeter, i.e.*

133

the metre of six feet (twelve syllables) used
in all the speeches in Greek tragedy.

Thus the *Oedipus Tyrannos* of Sophocles
begins:

᾿Ω τέκνα, Κάδμου του πάλαι νέα τροφὴ

and so on. It has twelve syllables, mostly
(iambics) as in our blank verse. But blank
verse has only ten syllables: 'I cannot tell
what you and other men.' If one adds two
syllables one gets the Greek iambic verse,
thus: 'I cannot tell what you and other
men believe.' The Chorus in the *Helena*
uses various rhythms such as are found in
the choruses of Greek tragedy:

> *Schweige, schweige,*
> *Missblickende, missredende du!*
> *Aus so grässlichen, einzahnigen*
> *Lippen was enthaucht wohl*
> *Solchem furchtbaren Greuelschlund!*

Then Mephistopheles, as the Phorkyad, when
Helen falls fainting, addresses her suddenly
in another measure—a longer verse, such as
is sometimes used by the Greek tragedians
and comedians when something new occurs
in the play. It is called a *tetrameter*, and
consists of fifteen syllables (mostly – ◡, called

AND GOETHE'S 'FAUST'

trochees). Thus, in Greek, οἱ γέροντες οἱ παλαιοὶ μεμφόμεσθα τῇ πόλει—and in German:

*Tritt hervor aus flüchtigen Wolken hohe Sonne dieses
   Tags—*

or the fine lines spoken by Helen:

*Doch es ziemet Königinnen, allen Menschen ziemt es
   wohl,
Sich zu fassen, zu ermannen, was auch drohend
   überrascht.*

When Faust appears he begins to speak at once in modern blank verse of ten syllables, such as we know in Milton and Shakespeare and Schiller. One might have expected him to speak in some earlier romantic measure, to have used perhaps the metre of the old Nibelungenlied, as in

*Es ist in alten Mähren wunders viel geseit,
Von Helcden lobebären, von grosser Arbeit,*

which is supposed to date from about 1150; or in Dante's *terza rima*, of about 1300, as

Nel mezzo del cammin di nostra vita.

But blank verse is after all the metre *par excellence* of the Renaissance, that is of the revival of Greek influence, and Goethe chose it for this reason.

THE FAUST-LEGEND

Now the Watchman Lynceus ('the keen-eyed,' as the word means—and you perhaps remember him as the watchman of the Argonauts on the good ship Argo) represents here the early pre-Renaissance poets of Italy and Provence and Germany—the Troubadours and Trouvères and Minne-singer, who were so surprised and dazzled by the sudden sunrise of the Renaissance with its wonderful new apparition of Greek art that they (as Lynceus in *Faust*) failed to announce its coming; and therefore Lynceus here speaks in a kind of early Troubadour metre, with *rime*. In classical poetry there is no rime. They did not like it; they even ridiculed it. For instance Cicero, the great orator, once tried to write poetry, and produced a line that said 'O fortunate Rome, when I was consul!' This was not only conceited of him but unfortunately the line contained a rime and this rime brought down an avalanche of ridicule on his head. 'O fortunatam natam me consule Romam' was this unfortunate line. Rime was probably first adopted by the monks in their medieval Latin hymns and was used by the Troubadours and early Italian poets when they began to write in

136

the vulgar tongue. Dante uses it in his
canzoni and sonnets and ballads, as well of
course as in his great poem. So it is quite
right to make Lynceus speak in rime.
Helen of course has never heard rime
before, and she turns to Faust and asks
him what it is that sounds so strange and
beautiful in this song of Lynceus; and she
wants to know how *she* too can learn the art.
So Faust tells her just to try and the rimes
will come of their own accord. But I will
quote the passage, for it is very pretty; and
I will add a rough translation.

> *Doch wünscht' ich Unterricht warum die Rede*
> *Des Manns mir seltsam klang, seltsam und*
>   *freundlich—*
> *Ein Ton scheint sich dem and'ren zu bequemen;*
> *Und hat ein Wort zum Ohre sich gesellt,*
> *Ein andres kommt, dem ersten liebzukosen. . . .*
> *So sage denn, wie spräch' ich auch so schön.*

FAUST. *Das ist gar leicht—es muss vom Herzen geh'n.*
> *Und wenn die Brust von Sehnsucht überfliesst*
> *Man sieht sich um, und fragt. . . .*

HELEN.   *wer mitgeniesst.*

FAUST. *Nun schaut der Geist nicht vorwärts, nicht*
>   *zuruck—*
> *Die Gegenwart allein . . .*

HELEN.   *ist unser Glück—*

FAUST. *Schatz ist sie, Hochgewinn, Besitz und Pfand.*
Bestätigung, wer gibt sie?

HELEN. *Meine Hand.*

(HELEN. *I fain would ask thee why the watchman's*
song
So strangely sounded—strange but beautiful.
Tones seemed to link themselves in harmony.
One word would come and nestle in the ear,
Then came another and caressed it there.
But say—how can I also learn the art?

FAUST. *Quite easily—one listens to one's heart,*
And when its longings seem too great to bear
We look around for one . . .

HELEN. *our joy to share.*

FAUST. *Not past nor future loving hearts can bless,*
The present—

HELEN. *is alone our happiness.*

FAUST. *Before the prize of beauty, lo I stand,*
But who assures the prize to me?

HELEN. *My hand!*)

In the midst of this life of chivalrous love
and romance Faust and Helen pass a period
of ecstatic bliss. But, as Goethe himself
found, such ecstasies are only a passing phase.
The end comes inevitably and suddenly.
A son is born to them, Euphorion by name
(the name of the winged son of Helen and
Achilles, according to one legend). He is

no common human child, As a butterfly
from its chrysalis he bursts at once into
fully developed existence. He is of enchant-
ing beauty but wild and capricious ; spurn-
ing the common earth he climbs ever higher
and higher amidst the mountain crags, sing-
ing ravishing melodies to his lyre. He
reaches the topmost crag and casts himself
into the air. A flame flickers upwards, and
the body of a beautiful youth 'in which one
seems to recognize a well-known form' falls
to the ground, at the feet of Faust and
Helen.

Euphorion symbolizes modern poetry,
and the well-known form is that of Byron.
For a moment the body lies there ; it then
dissolves in flame, which ascends to heaven,
and a voice is heard calling on Helen to
follow.

Yes, she must follow. As flame she
must return to her home in the Empyrean
—the home of ideal beauty and all other
ideals. However much we strive to realize
ideal beauty in art or in our lives, however
we may hold it to our hearts as a warm
and living possession, it always escapes our
grasp. The short-lived winged child of
poetic inspiration gleams but for a moment

and disappears, as a flame flickering back to its native empyrean. And she, the mother, she too must follow, leaving us alone to face the stern reality of life and of death.

In the embrace of Faust Helen melts away into thin air, leaving in his arms her robe and veil. These change into a cloud, which envelops him, raises him into the air and bears him also away. The Phorkyad picks up Euphorion's lyre and mantle; he steps forward and addresses the audience, assuring them that in the leavings of poetic genius he has got enough to fit out any number of modern poets, and is open to a bargain. He then swells up to a gigantic height, removes the Gorgon-mask, and reveals himself as Mephistopheles once more the northern modern devil; and the curtain falls.

When it rises for the Fourth Act we see a craggy mountain peak before us. A cloud approaches, and deposits Faust on the topmost crag. It lingers for a time, assuming wondrous shapes and then gradually melts away into the blue. Faust gazes at it. In its changing outlines he seems to discern first the regal forms of Olympian goddesses, of Juno, of Leda—then of Helen. But they fade away and, ere it disappears, the cloud assumes the likeness of that other half-forgotten human form which once had aroused in his heart that which he now feels to have been a love far truer and deeper than all his passion for ideal beauty—that 'swiftly felt and scarcely comprehended' love for a human heart which, as he now confesses to himself, 'had it been retained would have been his most precious possession.'

A seven-league boot now passes by—followed in hot haste by another. Out of the boots steps forth Mephistopheles. He asks contemptuously if Faust has had enough of heroines and all such ideal folly. He cannot understand why Faust is still dissatisfied with life. Surely he has seen enough of its pleasures. He advises him, if he is weary of court life, to build himself a Sultan's palace and harem and live in retirement—as Tiberius did on the island of Capri. 'Not so,' answers Faust. 'This world of earthly soil Still gives me room for greater action. I feel new strength for nobler toil—Toil that at length shall bring me satisfaction.'

He has determined to devote the rest of his

141

life to humanity, to the good of the human
race. It is a project with which Mephis-
topheles naturally has little sympathy. But
he is forced to acquiesce, and, being bound
to serve Faust even in this, he suggests a
plan. The young Kaiser is at present in
great difficulties. He is hard pressed by a
rival Emperor—a pretender to the Imperial
crown. Mephisto will by his magic arts
secure the Kaiser the victory over this
pretender, and then Faust will claim as
recompense a tract of country bordering on
the ocean. Here by means of canals and
dykes, dug and built by demonic powers,
Faust is to reclaim from the sea a large
region of fertile country and to found a
kind of model republic, where peace and
prosperity and every social and political
blessing shall find a home. The plan is
carried out. At the summons of Mephis-
topheles appear three gigantic warriors by
whose help the battle is won, and Faust
gains his reward—the stretch of land on
the shore of the ocean. And he is not the
only gainer. The Archbishop takes the
opportunity of extracting far more valuable
concessions of land from the young Kaiser
as penance for his having associated himself

with powers of darkness. The prelate even extracts the promise of tithes and dues from all the land still unclaimed by Faust. As Mephistopheles aptly remarks, the Church seems to have a good digestion.

Many years are now supposed to elapse. Faust has nearly completed his task of expelling the sea and founding his ideal state. What had been a watery waste is now like the garden of Eden in its luxuriant fertility. Thousands of industrious happy mortals have found in this new country a refuge and a home. Ships, laden with costly wares, throng the ports. On an eminence overlooking the scene stands the castle of Faust, and not far off are a cottage and a chapel. On this scene the last act opens. A wanderer enters. He is seeking the cottage which once used to stand here, on the very brink of the ocean. It was here that he was shipwrecked: here, on this very spot, the waves had cast him ashore: here stands still the cottage of the poor old peasant and his wife who had rescued him from death. But now the sea is sparkling in the blue distance and beneath him spreads the new country with its waving cornfields. He enters the cottage and is

welcomed by the poor old couple (to whom
Goethe has given the names Philemon and
Baucis, the old peasant and his wife who,
according to the Greek legend, were the
only Phrygians who offered hospitality to
Zeus, the King of the Gods, as he was
wandering about in disguise among mortals).

Faust comes out on to the garden terrace
of his castle. He is now an old man—close
upon a hundred years of age. He gazes
with a feeling of happiness and satisfaction
at the scene that lies below him—the wide
expanse of fertile land, the harbours and
canals filled with shipping. Suddenly the
bell in the little chapel begins to ring for
Vespers.

Faust's happiness is in a moment changed
into bitterness and anger. This cottage,
this chapel, this little plot of land are as
thorns in his side: they are the Naboth's
vineyard which he covets and which alone
interferes with his territorial rights. He
has offered large sums of money, but the
peasant will not give up his home.

Mephistopheles and his helpers (the same
three gigantic supernatural beings who took
part in the battle) appear. Faust vents his
anger and chagrin with regard to the peasant

144

and the irritating ding-dong-dell of the vesper bell. He commissions Mephistopheles to persuade the peasant to take the money and to make him turn out of his wretched hut. Mephistopheles and his mates go to carry out the order. A few moments later flames are seen to rise from the cottage and chapel. Mephistopheles returns to relate that the peasant and the wanderer proved obstinate: in the scuffle the wanderer had been killed; the cottage had caught fire, and old Philemon and his wife had both died of terror.

Faust turns upon Mephistopheles with fierce anger and curses him. 'I meant exchange!' he exclaims. 'I meant to *make it good with money!* I meant not robbery and murder. I curse the deed. Thou, not I, shalt bear the guilt.'

Here I do not find it easy to follow Faust's line of argument. Fair exchange is certainly said to be no robbery—but this theory of 'making everything good with money' is one which the average foreigner is apt to attribute especially to the average Britisher, and it does not raise Faust in one's estimation. I suppose he thinks he is doing the poor old couple a blessing in

disguise by ejecting them out of their
wretched hovel and presenting them with a
sum of money of perhaps ten times its value.

Possibly Goethe means it to be a specimen
of the kind of mistake that well-meaning
theoretical philanthropists are apt to commit
with their Juggernaut of Human Progress.
Faust is filled with great philanthropic ideas
—but perhaps he is a little apt to ignore
the individual. Anyhow his better self
'meant not robbery and murder' and is
perhaps quite justified in cursing its demonic
companion and giving him the whole of
the guilt.

The scene changes. It is midnight. Faust,
sleepless and restless, is pacing the hall in
his castle. Outside, on the castle terrace,
appear four phantom shapes clothed as
women in dusky robes. They are Want,
Guilt, Care, and Need. The four grey sisters
make halt before the castle. In hollow,
awe-inspiring tones they recite in turn their
dirge-like strains: they chant of gathering
clouds and darkness, and of their brother—
Death. They approach the door of the
castle hall. It is shut. Within lives a rich
man, and none of them may enter, not even
Guilt — none save only Care. She slips

through the keyhole. Faust feels her un-
seen presence.

'Is any one here?' he asks.

'The question demandeth *Yes!*'

'And thou . . . who art thou?'

'' Tis enough that I am here.'

'Avaunt!'

'I am where I should be.'

Faust defies the phantom. She, standing
there invisible, recites in tones like the knell
of a passing-bell the fate of a man haunted
by Care: how he gradually loses sight of his
high ideals and wanders blindly amid the
maze of worldly illusions—how he loses
faith and joy—how he starves amidst plenty
—has no certain aim in life—burdening him-
self and others, breathing air that chokes
him, living a phantom life—a dead thing,
a death-in-life—supporting himself on a hope
that is no hope, but despair—never content,
never resigned, never knowing what he
should do, or what he himself wishes.

'Accursed spectres!' exclaims Faust.
'Thus ye ever treat the human race. From
demons, I know, it is scarce possible to free
oneself. But *thy* power, O Care—so great
and so insidious though it be, I will *not*
recognize it!'

147

'So *feel* it now!' answers the phantom. 'Throughout their whole existence men are mostly *blind*—So let it be at last with thee!'

She approaches, breathes in Faust's face, and he is struck blind.

He stands there dazed and astounded. Thick darkness has fallen upon him. At last he speaks:

Still deeper seems the night to surge around me,
But in my inmost spirit all is light.
I'll rest not till the finished work has crown'd me.
God's promise—that alone doth give me might.

He hastens forth, groping his way in blindness, to call up his workmen. His life is ending and he must end his work. It is midnight, but the light within him makes him think the day has dawned. In the courtyard there are awaiting him Mephistopheles and a band of Lemurs—horrible skeleton-figures with shovels and torches. They are digging his grave. Faust mistakes the sound for that of his workmen, and incites them to labour. He orders the overseer, Mephistopheles, to press on with the work . . . to finish the last great moat —or 'Graben.'

148

AND GOETHE'S 'FAUST'

'*Man spricht*,' answers Mephistopheles *sotto voce*,

> '*Man spricht, wie man mir Nachricht gab,*
> *Von keinem* Graben—*doch vom Grab.*'

It is no moat, no Graben, that is now being dug, but a grave—a Grab.

Standing on the very verge of his grave, Faust, reviewing the memories of his long life, feels that *at last*, though old and blind, with no more hopes in earthly existence, he has won peace and happiness in having worked for others and in having given other human beings a measure of independence and of that true liberty and happiness which are gained only by honest toil. He alone truly *possesses* and can *enjoy* who has made a thing his own by earning it.

> *Yes, to this thought I hold with firm persistence;*
> *The last result of wisdom stamps it true;*
> *He only earns his freedom and existence*
> *Who daily conquers them anew.*
> *And such a throng I fain would see—*
> *Would stand on a free soil, with people free.*

Standing there, on the very edge of his new-dug grave he blesses the present moment and bids it stay. The fatal words are spoken and according to the compact his life must end.

149

He sinks lifeless to the ground. The Lemurs lay him in the open grave. Mephistopheles, triumphant, looks on and exclaims:

No joy could sate him, no delight suffice.
To grasp at empty shades was his endeavour.
The latest, poorest emptiest moment—this—
Poor fool, he tried to hold it fast for ever.
Me he resisted in such vigorous wise;
But Time is lord—and there the old man lies!
The clock stands still.

'Stands still,' repeats a voice from heaven, 'still, silent, as the midnight.' 'It is finished,' says Mephistopheles. 'Nay. 'Tis but past,' answers the voice. 'Past!' exclaims Mephistopheles; 'how *past* and yet not *finished?*' . . . He is enraged at the suspicion that life, though past, may not be *finished*—that Faust's human soul may *yet* elude that hell to which he destines it . . . that of annihilation.

The Lemurs group themselves round the grave and chant with hollow voices, such as skeletons may be supposed to have, a funeral dirge. Meantime Mephistopheles is busy summoning his demons to keep watch over the dead body, lest the soul should escape like a mouse, or flicker up to heaven in a little

150

flamelet. Hideous forms of demons, fat and thin, with straight and crooked horns, tusked like boars and with claws like vultures, come thronging in, while the jaw of hell opens itself, showing in the distance the fiery city of Satan.

At this moment a celestial glory is seen descending from heaven and voices of angels are heard singing a song of triumph and salvation. They approach ever nearer— Mephistopheles rages and curses, but in vain. They come ever onward, casting before them roses, the flowers of Paradise, which burst in flame and scorch the demons, who, rushing at their angelic adversaries with their hellish prongs and forks and launching vainly their missiles of hell-fire, are hurled back by an invisible power and gradually driven off the stage, plunging in hideous ruin and combustion down headlong into the jaws of hell.

Mephistopheles alone remains, foaming in impotent rage. He is surrounded by the choir of white-robed angels. He stands powerless there, while they gather to themselves Faust's immortal part and ascend amidst songs of triumph to heaven.

Some of us, perhaps most of us—in certain

THE FAUST-LEGEND

moods at least—feel inclined to close the book here, as we do with *Hamlet* at the words 'the rest is silence.' And this feeling is all the stronger when we have witnessed the stage decorator's pasteboard heaven, where Apostles and Fathers are posed artistically in rather perilous situations amid rocks and pine-trees, or balance themselves with evident anxiety mid-air on pendent platforms representing clouds. Altogether this stage-heaven is a very uncomfortable and depressing kind of place.

But when read in Goethe's poem and regarded as an allegorical vision the scene has a certain impressive grandeur, and some of the hymns of adoration and triumph are of exceeding beauty.

This Scene in Heaven opens with the songs of the three great Fathers, the Pater Ecstaticus, Pater Profundus, and Pater Seraphicus, symbolizing the three stages of human aspiration, namely ecstasy, contemplation and seraphic love. The Seraphic Father is of course St. Francis of Assisi. In heaven, as he did on earth, he sings of the revelation of Eternal Love.

Angels are now seen ascending and bear-

152

ing Faust's immortal part, and as they rise
they sing :

> *The noble spirit now is free*
> *And saved from evil scheming.*
> *Whoe'er aspires unweariedly*
> *Is not beyond redeeming,*
> *And if he feels the grace of Love*
> *That from on high is given*
> *The blessed hosts that wait above*
> *Shall welcome him to heaven.*

His yet unawakened soul is greeted by the
heavenly choirs and by the three penitents,
the Magdalene, the woman of Samaria and
St. Mary of Egypt.

Then appears 'timidly stealing forth
the glorified form of her who on earth wa:
called Gretchen. In words that remind one
of her former prayer of remorse and despair
in the Cathedral she offers her petition to the
Virgin :

> *O Mary, hear me!*
> *From realms supernal*
> *Of light eternal*
> *Incline thy countenance upon my bliss!*
> *My loved, my lover,*
> *His trials over*
> *In yonder world, returns to me in this.*

153

THE FAUST-LEGEND

The Virgin in her glory appears. She addresses Gretchen:

Come, raise thyself to higher spheres !
For he will follow when he feels thee near.

Gretchen soars up to the higher heaven, and the soul of Faust, now awakening to consciousness, rises also heavenward following her, while the chorus of angels sings, in words the beauty and power of which I dare not mar by translation, telling how all things earthly are but a vision, and how in heaven the imperfect is made perfect and the inconceivable wins attainment, and how that which leads us upward and heavenward is immortal love.

Alles Vergängliche
Ist nur ein Gleichnis ;
Das Unzulängliche,
Hier wird's Ereignis ;
Das Unbeschreibliche,
Hier ist's getan ;
Das Ewig-weibliche
Zieht uns hinan.

LaVergne, TN USA
18 January 2010
170427LV00002B/13/A